Epistemic Logic

Epistemic Logic

A SURVEY OF THE
LOGIC OF KNOWLEDGE

Nicholas Rescher

UNIVERSITY OF PITTSBURGH PRESS

Published by the University of Pittsburgh Press, Pittsburgh, Pa., 15260
Copyright © 2005, University of Pittsburgh Press
Manufactured in the United States of America
Printed on acid-free paper
10 9 8 7 6 5 4 3 2 1

Library of Congress Cataloging-in-Publication Data

Rescher, Nicholas.
Epistemic logic : a survey of the logic of knowledge / Nicholas Rescher.
p. cm.
Includes bibliographical references and index.
ISBN 0-8229-4246-1 (alk. paper)
1. Epistemics. 2. Logic. 3. Knowledge, Theory of. I. Title.
BC21.E64R47 2005
160—dc22
2004021645

For Neil Tennant

Contents

	Preface	vii
1.	Setting the Stage	1
2.	Basic Principles	8
3.	Deductivity and Knowledge Ampliation	14
4.	Metaknowledge	20
5.	For Aught That Someone Knows	25
6.	Group Knowledge	30
7.	Propositional versus Interrogative Knowledge	35
8.	Collective versus Distributive Knowledge and Knower Limitedness	42
9.	Modality	49
10.	Problems of Epistemic Democracy	55
11.	Possibility and Conceivability	58
12.	Unknowability	62
13.	Fitch's Theorem and Its Consequences	66
14.	Finite and Infinite Knowers	71
15.	Vagrant Predicates and Noninstantiability	76
16.	Unanswerable Questions and Insolubilia	85
17.	Unknowable Truth	94
18.	Implications of Cognitive Limitation	100
	Appendix 1: A Survey of Thesis Acceptability	105
	Appendix 2: On Quantifying Knowledge (and the Gulf Between Linguistic Truth and Objective Fact)	109
	Notes	125
	Bibliography	135
	Index	139

Preface

Not long ago I was invited to contribute a sketch of epistemic logic offering a general survey of philosophical logic to *A Companion to Philosophical Logic* (Oxford University Press). When preparing this piece, it struck me that there actually is no synoptic account of the field. Despite a great many articles in scholarly journals dealing with special topics in epistemic logic, there does not exist a text that puts the pieces together in a systematic exposition of the field that connects it with the issues of philosophical epistemology. My aim here is to fill this gap. The topic is of sufficiently wide interest—not only to logicians but also to philosophers, cognitive scientists, information scientists, artificial intelligence researchers, and others—that students need and deserve a helping hand in securing convenient access to this domain.

I am grateful for the helpfulness of various individuals: the students in my Epistemology course in the fall of 2001—especially, Dane Roberts—for the opportunity their questions have afforded me to work out this presentation of the relevant ideas; my Pittsburgh colleagues Joseph Camp and Anil Gupta for numerous helpful suggestions; and to my assistant, Estelle Burris, for her patience and competence.

Epistemic Logic

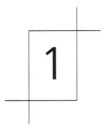

Setting the Stage

The Idea of Epistemic Logic

Epistemic logic is that branch of philosophical logic that seeks to formalize the logic of discourse about knowledge. Its object is to articulate and clarify the general principles of reasoning about claims to and attributions of knowledge—to elucidate their inferential implications and consequences. In pursuing this goal, it deals principally with propositional knowledge (along the lines of "Smith knows *that* coal is black") and secondarily also with interrogative knowledge (along the lines of "Jones knows *where* the treasure is buried and *who* put it there").[1] It is the object of this book to give an overview of the discipline by setting out in a formalized manner the general principles for reasoning about such matters.

The History of Epistemic Logic

Epistemic logic is a product of the second half of the twentieth century. After the preliminary work of Rudolf Carnap's deliberations about belief sentences,[2] epistemic logic was launched in an important 1948 paper by the Polish logician Jerzy Łoś.[3] Łoś developed what he called a logic of "belief" or "acceptance" based on an operator Lxp for "the individual x believes (or is committed to) the proposition p," for which he stipulated axiomatic rules substantially akin to those to be specified for the knowledge operator to be introduced below. A spate of publication during the 1950s by such logicians as Alonzo Church, Arthur Prior, Hilary Putnam, G. H. von Wright, and the present writer further extended the range of relevant deliberations. During the 1960s various authors carried matters forward, with the first book on the topic (by Jaakko Hintikka) appearing in 1962. Since then there has been a small but steady stream of work in the field. (For details, see the bibliography.)

Fundamentals of Notation

The present treatment of epistemic logic undertakes the construction of a deductively formalized system **s** that is adequate for this purpose. As is often the case with axiomatic treatments, the present discussion illustrates how a modest set of basic assumptions provides a great deal of instructive information about the conceptual anatomy of the idea at issue.

Use will be made here of the familiar resources of propositional and quantificational logic supplemented by the machinery of quantified modal logic. All of the following symbols will accordingly be used in the standard way:

$\sim$, &, $\vee$, $\supset$, and $\equiv$ for the familiar propositional connectives

$\forall$ and $\exists$ for universal and existential quantification

$\square$ and $\lozenge$ for the modalities of necessity and possibility

Additionally, the following notational conventions will be employed:

Kxp ("x knows that p")

K^*xp ("p is derivable from propositions that x knows")

$x, y, z, \ldots$ as variables for knowers: intelligent individual (or possibly groups thereof)

$p, q, r, \ldots$ as variables for propositions (contentions to the effect "that such-and-such is the case")

$t, t', t'', \ldots$ as variables for specifically true propositions (note that

$(\forall t)F(t)$ amounts to $(\forall p)(p \supset F(p))$ and $(\exists t)F(t)$ amounts to $(\exists p)(p \,\&\, F(p))$, F being an arbitrary propositional function
$u, u', u'', \ldots$ as variables for objects of consideration or discussion
$F, G, H, \ldots$ as variables for properties or features objects or of propositions
$S, S', S'', \ldots$ as variables for sets of objects or propositions
$Q, Q', Q'', \ldots$ as variables for questions

The quantificational logic at work here is type differentiated: p, q, r, and so on stand for propositions x, y, z, and so on for knowers and so on. One could, in theory, employ a single class of variable α, β, γ and so on, and then render

$(\forall x)Fx$ as $(\forall \alpha)(\alpha \in K \supset F\alpha)$,
  where K represents the set of knowers,
$(\exists p)Gp$ as $(\exists \alpha)(\alpha \in P \,\&\, G\alpha)$,
  where P represents the set of propositions,

and the like. But this more elaborate style of presentation would make our formulations needlessly complicated and less easily read. It should be noted that the various domains at issue (knowers, propositions, truths, and the like) are all nonempty, so that the inference from "all" to "some" is appropriate in all cases.

Certain special symbols will be employed as follows:
$\vdash p$ for "p is a thesis of our system (**s**)"
$\Vdash p$ for $\vdash (\forall x)Kxp$
$p \vdash q$ for $\vdash p \supset q$
$p \Vdash q$ for $\vdash (\forall x)Kxp \supset Kxq)$
$p \,@\, Q$ for "p answers the question Q"

The symbol $\vdash$ will also be called upon to serve as an index of entailment through the following equivalence:
$p \vdash q$ iff $\vdash (p \supset q)$

Since the antecedent p may disaggregate into the conjunction of a series of propositions, $p_1, p_2, \ldots p_n$, this stipulation renders our system subject to what is standardly called the deduction theorem, on the basis of the following equivalence:

$$p_1, p_2, \ldots, p_n \vdash q \text{ if and only if } p_1, p_2, \ldots, p_{n-1} \vdash p_n \supset q.$$

With propositional knowledge of matters of fact, the basic unit of assertion will be a statement of the form "x knows that p" (Kxp). Such propositional knowledge is a matter of a relationship—a *cognitive* relationship—between a person and a true proposition. And just as for an otherwise unidentified individual x one can uniformly substitute the name of any individual, so for an otherwise unidentified proposition p one can uniformly substitute any other. The use of variables thus affords a gateway to generality by providing for substitution. For example, since it obtains as a general principle that

If Kxp, then p,

one automatically secures a vast range of such other assertions as

If $Ky(p \& q)$, then $p \& q$,

which results from the preceding via the substitutions y/x and $(p \& q)/p$.

Recourse to symbolic representation enables us to achieve greater precision. For instance, in ordinary language "x does not know that p" is equivocal as between $\sim Kxp$ and $p \& \sim Kxp$, which would be more accurately formulated as "p, and x does not know it."

Theses of the System

As already mentioned, $\vdash$ here serves as an assertion symbol indicating that what follows qualifies as a general principle of the system of epistemic logic (**s**) that is under construction. By convention its employment conveys implicit universality for any free variables. Thus,

$\vdash Kxp \supset p$

asserts that $(\forall x)(\forall p)(Kxp \supset p)$ holds in our system. A proposition that qualifies as a thesis of the system should be seen as being true on logico-conceptual grounds alone. Its validation will rest entirely on the specification of the terms of reference that are employed and thus on the conventions of meaning and usage that are being adopted. These theses accordingly serve to specify the conception of *knowledge* that is to be at issue. And since a "logic" of knowledge must deal in general principles, it is the establishment or refutation of such conceptually grounded generalizations that concern us at present. What is at work here is in fact a somewhat delicate reciprocal feedback process. A certain particular conception of knowledge guides the construction of our epistemic system. And the theses of this system define and precisify the particular conception of knowledge that is at issue.

In dealing with knowledge and its "logic" we are not, of course, functioning in a realm of total abstraction, as would be the case with "pure" (rather than applied) mathematical or theoretical logic. Instead, we are dealing with the resources of intelligent beings (not necessarily members of *Homo sapiens*) operating substantially within the limits imposed by the realities of this world of ours. Accordingly, the "facts of life" that reflect the cognitive situation of such beings and the conditions that define their situation in this world represent the ultimately factual (rather than purely theoretical) circumstances that a logic of knowledge as such will have to reflect. In particular, knowers have to be construed as finite beings with finite capacities, even though reality, nature, has an effectively infinite cognitive depth in point of detail, in that no matter how elaborate our characterizations of the real, there is always more to be said.[4] The reality of it is that epistemic logic is an applied logic and its theses, being geared to salient feature of the established concept of knowledge, stand correlative to the ways in which we actually do talk and think about the matter.

Propositions as Objects of Knowledge

There is nothing problematic about saying "*p*, but *x* does not know (or believe) it." But in the special case of *x* = oneself (the assertor), this otherwise viable locution is impracticable. This discrepant state of affairs has become known as "Moore's paradox" after G. E. Moore, who first puzzled over it.[5] Of course, there would be nothing amiss about saying "I surmise (conjecture, suspect) that *p* but do not actually know

(or confidently believe) it." But in making a flat-out, unqualified statement we stand subject to the ground rule that this purports knowing
the truth of the matter, so that in going on to add "but I do not know
(or believe) it" to an assertion of ours, we take the inconsistent line of
giving with one hand what we take away with the other. Our categor-
ical (that is, unqualified) assertions stand subject to an implicit claim
to truth and knowledge, and we thus authorize the inference from asserting p both to Kip and to p itself. Accordingly, when our system **s** is
held to make an explicit assertion, this will be something that we ourselves purport to know, so that we then have it that $\vdash p$ entails $(\exists x)Kxp$.

In general, claims to knowledge regarding individual objects or
collections thereof can be reformulated with the machinery of propositional knowledge by means of quantification. Thus, consider
    "x knows the identity of Jack the Ripper":
        $(\exists p)$ (p identifies who Jack the Ripper was & Kxp)
    "x knows the major features of London's topography":
        $(\forall p)$ (p states a major feature of London's topography $\supset Kxp$)[6]

Such statements about someone's knowledge of individual objects can
be reduced to propositional knowledge by employing either
        $(\exists p)(p @ Q \text{ & } Kxp)$

or
        $(\forall p)(p @ Q \supset Kxp)$

when $p @ Q$ abbreviates "p answers the question Q."

By and large, propositional knowledge represents a resource by
whose means the other principal versions of the concept of knowledge
can be recast and represented. However, some knowledge is not
propositionally reducible, specifically, know-how of a certain sort. For
we have to distinguish between

    performatory know-how: x knows how to do A in the sense that x
        can do A; and
    procedural know-how: x knows how A is done in the sense that x
        can spell out instructions for doing A.

The second sort of know-how is clearly a matter of propositional knowledge—that x knows that A can be done by doing such-and-such things; for example, x knows that people swim by moving their arms and legs in a certain cycle of rhythmic motions. But, of course, x can know how A is done without being able to do A—that is, without x having the performatory skills that enable x to do A. (For example, x may know *that* a certain result is produced when a text is translated from one language to another without actually knowing *how* to make such a translation.) And, therefore, while propositional reduction is practicable with respect to *procedural* know-how, such a reduction will not be practicable with respect to *performatory* know-how, seeing that people are clearly able to do all sorts of things (catch balls, remember faces) without being able to spell out a process or procedure for doing so.[7]

All the same, the different modes of knowledge are inextricably interconnected. To know (propositionally) *that* a cat is on the mat one must know (adverbially) *what* a cat is. And this knowledge rests on knowing how to tell cats from kangaroos.

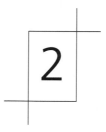

2

Basic Principles

Acceptance and Assertion

The distinction between four modes of propositional acceptance/assertion will be serviceable in characterizing the present system of epistemic logic (**s**):

Type 1: $\Vdash p$, that is, iff $\vdash (\forall x)Kxp$. This represents "obvious knowledge" coordinate with acceptance by our epistemic system (**s**) of *p* as something *universally recognized* among the knowers at issue.

Type 2: $\vdash p$, that is, iff $K\mathbf{s}p$. On this basis we propose to accept *p* as part of our epistemic system (**s**), itself now regarded as a "knower" of sorts.[1] Such acceptance represents "patent knowledge" coordinate with acceptance as certain on epistemico-logical grounds. (It, accordingly, includes the theses of both epistemic and standard logic.)

Type 3: p, that is, Kip, where $i =$ oneself. Note that, as already discussed in chapter 1, when one makes a flat-out assertion of *p*, one claims to know it, so that asserting *p* comes to claiming *Kip*.

Type 4: $\ast p$, that is, a qualified assertion of *p*. This represents "merely accepted belief" coordinate with a tentative or provisional acceptance as true, conceivably on the basis of conjecture rather than actual knowledge.

In the fourth case we do indeed regard the proposition in question as acceptable but without claiming assured *knowledge* of the matter. A type-4 assertion has to be seen as a truth that is not actually known but only (and perhaps hesitatingly) endorsed. Such theses may be surmised or presumed, regarded as plausibly putative truths—as was the case with the thesis "There are mountains on the far side of the moon" in the cognitive state of the art of the nineteenth century. What is at issue is a tentatively adopted mere belief that, as such, contrasts decidedly with actual knowledge. In claiming *p* in the mode of ✳-assertability we do no more than to characterize it as a putative truth, rather than as one that is deemed to be certifiable as such. (Such theses will not form part of one's purported knowledge, let alone of the assertions of **s** itself.) The existence of the fourth level of assertion is a reminder that epistemology is broader than the theory of *knowledge*. For matters of presumption, conjecture, reasonable belief, and plausible assertability also clearly fall within its purview.

On this basis, then, all four of these modes of acceptance do indeed convey a commitment—an *assertion*. A claim that *p* is the case obtains in every instance, but with different epistemic modalities—conjecture, plausible supposition, or the like. Such tentative endorsements say that something is true, all right, but in a substantially less firm and confident tone of voice.

It deserves noting that one can maintain that

$$✳(p \ \& \sim(\exists x)Kxp)$$

without self-contradiction. The claim "*p* is presumably true, although no one actually knows it (for sure)" is viable. But, of course,

$$Ki(p \ \& \sim(\exists x)Kxp)$$

is self-contradicting in claiming both that one knows *p* and that nobody does. Accordingly,

$$p \ \& \sim(\exists x)Kxp$$

can be maintained as a type-3 assertion but not as a type-2 one (let alone a type 1 one).

Some Fundamental Principles

Four principles will play a leading role in the system **s** that we are engaged in elaborating:

1. *Knower capacity:* We are dealing with actual knowers, individuals who know at least *something:*

   $\vdash (\forall x)(\exists p)Kxp$

2. *Knower limitation:* We are dealing with knowers of limited capacity, none of whom are omniscient:

   $\vdash (\forall x)(\exists p)(p \mathbin{\&} \sim Kxp)$

Thus, a godlike being who knows everything is left out of the range of present concern. This does not, of course, mean that omniscience itself is a logical impossibility. It is merely excluded as a viable prospect for the particular conception of knowledge and knowers that is at issue in the present context of deliberation.

3. *Veracity:* Whatever is actually known by someone will have to be the case. Where we credit knowledge we must credit truth as well: there is no such thing as a *knowledge* of falsehoods; that sort of thing would have to be classed as merely *putative* knowledge.

   $\vdash Kxp \supset p$

Actual knowledge, in short, must be veridical.

4. *Conjunctivity:* Knowers have the (rather minimal) competence of being able to "put two and two together." When a knower knows two facts separately, the knower knows them conjunctively. If *Kxp* and *Kxq,* then *Kx*(*p* & *q*):

   $\vdash (Kxp \mathbin{\&} Kxq) \supset Kx(p \mathbin{\&} q)$

Thesis (4) is controversial. What renders it problematic is that its analogue clearly fails for merely probable (that is, less than certain) propositions: a conjunction of probable truths need not itself be probable.[2] But, of course, knowledge should be certain. And in any case the present discussion construes "knowing" in a generous sense of potential accessibility that goes somewhat beyond the realities of ordinary performance. The thesis at issue is thus less a consequence of theoretically geared principles than an artifact of the particular sense of *knowledge* at work in the present systematization of the concept.

Moreover, the converse of thesis 4 also obtains:

5. *Converse conjunctivity: Knowledge is disaggregative:* what is known conjunctively is also known separately:

$\vdash Kx(p \ \& \ q) \supset (Kxp \ \& \ Kxq)$

Two important consequences follow from the preceding principles:

Knowledge is consistent: If *Kxp* and *Kyq*, then *p* is bound to be compatible with *q*.

This follows from *veracity* and *conjunctivity* in view of the overall consistency of the truth. For *Kxp* and *Kyq* yields *p* & *q*. Accordingly,

If *Kxp* & *Kxq*, then never $p \vdash \sim q$.

Falsehoods are unknowable. Knowledge requires conformity to fact, and falsehoods are not factual.

Accordingly, falsehoods cannot be known: If *p* is false, then no one can know that *p*: If $\sim p$, then $\sim (\exists x) Kxp$, or equivalently: If $(\exists x) Kxp$, then *p*. This can be demonstrated via thesis 3, *veracity*. An unknown truth is a real loss, but the unknowability of falsehoods is simply a matter of excluding error from the cognitive realm.

We must, of course, credit our knowers with the modest intelligence requisite for grasping certain elemental truths. Thus, the *p*-universalized thesis

$Kx(p \lor \sim p)$

is quite appropriate, unlike the *p*-universalized thesis

$Kxp \lor Kx\sim p$.

It is one thing to know *that* one of several propositions is true according to $K(p \lor q)$, but it is something quite different to know *which* of several propositions is true according to $Kxp \lor Kxq$.

One helpful way of looking at the matter is that these various principles are definitively constitutive of the sense of knowledge at issue here through serving to spell out its conceptual ramifications.

Some Theses about Knowers and Knowledge

Consider the following four theses about knowers:

(A)
I. $(\forall x)(\forall t)Kxt$
II. $(\forall x)(\exists t)Kxt$
III. $(\exists x)(\forall t)Kxt$
IV. $(\exists x)(\exists t)Kxt$

Here thesis IV, that somebody knows something, is, of course, at odds with radical skepticism.

By the rules of quantificational logic we have

where the arrows represent entailment relationships. Since here we are concerned with imperfect knowers of limited capacity and prescind from an omniscient knower, we reject thesis III and hence thesis I in its wake. And since we are concerned with actual knowers, we accept thesis II and hence thesis IV in its wake. Accordingly, our stance toward the four theses at issue is $- + - +$.

It is informative also to consider the situation in regard to ignorance:

(B)
I. $(\forall x)(\forall t)\sim Kxt$ ($\equiv$ not AIV)
II. $(\forall x)(\exists t)\sim Kxt$ ($\equiv$ not AIII)
III. $(\exists x)(\forall t)\sim Kxt$ ($\equiv$ not AII)
IV. $(\exists x)(\exists t)\sim Kxt$ ($\equiv$ not AI)

Given our rejection of skepticism, we reject thesis I, and since our knowers are specifically *limited* knowers, we accept thesis II and thus thesis IV in its wake. And since actual knowers are at issue, we must reject thesis III and thus thesis I in its wake. The resulting acceptance profile for the propositions of spectrum (B) is once again: $- + - +$.

Consider further the (A)-analogous spectrum of t-first theses:

(C)
    I. $(\forall t)(\forall x)Kxt\ (\equiv AI)$
    II. $(\forall t)(\exists x)Kxt$
    III. $(\exists t)(\forall x)Kxt$
    IV. $(\exists t)(\exists x)Kxt\ (\equiv AIV)$

Subsequent discussion will show that thesis II must be rejected. But thesis III is acceptable given such inevitable items of knowledge as "Somebody knows something." We accordingly have the acceptance profile $- - + +$.

Finally, consider the (B)-analogous spectrum of t-first theses:

(D)
    I. $(\forall t)(\forall x)\sim Kxt\ (\equiv BI)$
    II. $(\forall t)(\exists x)\sim Kxt$
         or equivalently $\sim(\exists t)(\forall x)Kxt$
         $(\equiv \text{not CIII})$
    III. $(\exists t)(\forall x)\sim Kxt$
         or equivalently $\sim(\forall t)(\exists x)Kxt$
         $(\equiv \text{not CII})$
    IV. $(\exists t)(\exists x)\sim Kxt\ (\equiv BIV)$

In view of the previously indicated relationships, we here have once more the acceptance profile $- - + +$.

The eight acceptable theses among these four spectra represent some of the most basic facts of epistemic logic.[3] They are a direct consequence of the sorts of "knowers" we suppose to be at issue in these deliberations and thus obtain with a sort of hypothetical necessity.

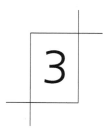

Deductivity and Knowledge Ampliation

Available Knowledge

In developing a system of epistemic logic one needs to be able to engage in deductive inference not only on one's own account but also on account of the knowers at issue in the deliberations. To this end we shall adopt the following thesis:

Deductivity principle: If Kxp and $Kx(p \vdash q)$, then Kxq.

This thesis credits knowers with the known consequence of known facts. It emerges on this basis that the conception of knowledge at issue with the knowledge operator K is what might be characterized as *available* knowledge—that is, knowledge that need not be explicitly avowed as such by the knowers in question but is available to them through their own inferential resources—that is, those inferential processes they know to obtain. All this is simply an artifact of the way in which the idea of knowing is being construed in the setting of the present deliberations.

Accessible Knowledge and Logical Omniscience

One can also introduce a yet more generous knowledge operator K^* subject to the following thesis:

Weak deductivity principle: If K^*xp and $p \vdash q$, then K^*xq,

or, equivalently,

If $p \vdash q$, then $K^*xp \vdash K^*xq$.

This stretches the idea of tacit knowledge to its limit because we now credit our knowers with an implicit knowledge of whatever is deductively encompassed in their knowledge—and not just via those deductive relationships that the knowers actually know about, but via whatever deductive relations there are, even where these are not recognized by the knowers. However convenient this sort of "knowledge" is from a logician's point of view, it is totally unrealistic as a representation of the sort of knowledge that figures in everyday-language discourse about this idea.[1]

In fact, what is at issue here is not knowledge proper but rather *available information.* For with respect to *this* over-generous mode of "knowledge" we credit our knowers with "logical omniscience" and in particular we must now accept the principle,

Whenever $\vdash p$, then $\vdash K^*xp$,

which certainly does not hold for the standard mode of knowledge represented by K. All of our knowers are thus seen as K^*-omniscient with respect to all the facts of logic. (To be sure, when we allow our system **s** itself to count as a knower, then this sort of knowledge will be at issue, seeing that the system itself "knows" all of its theorems.) However, while such an over-generous conception of knowledge construes the idea in a somewhat unrealistic way, nevertheless, it does have a potentially useful part to play in epistemic deliberations. For when it comes to inquiry into the *limits of knowledge,* this conception will prove serviceable. For if and when there are any facts that cannot be known in even this over-generous sense of the term, then such facts are thereby securely emplaced outside the realm of the knowable at large.

Machinery of Ampliation: Obvious Inference and Universal Knowledge

The philosophical tradition is replete with items of knowledge that are supposedly universal: the *axiometa* and *kataleptic* perceptions of the Stoics, Descartes' clear and distinct perceptions of the mind, Husserl's *evident* propositions, G. E. Moore's patent truths ("There are human hands"), and the like. And there are certainly some elemental theses that would seem to qualify as virtually inevitable candidates for universal knowledge:

- Something exists.
- There are some truths.
- Somebody knows something.
- Nobody knows everything.

Such items of information may be taken as cognitively inescapable facts. And some among them may be regarded as so fundamental that they qualify as theses of our epistemic system.

Whereas $\vdash$ represents a system-bound cognitive standing, $\Vdash$ will here represent "obvious" knowledge—that is, knowledge that is universal for our population of knowers—with $\Vdash p$ amounting to $\vdash (\forall x) Kxp$. A plausible example of such universal knowledge is afforded by such theses as "somebody knows something"—symbolically, $(\exists y)(\exists p) Kyp$—which reflects our system's rejection of radical skepticism. The claim at issue here comes to

$$\Vdash (\exists y)(\exists p) Kyp$$

or, equivalently,

$$\vdash (\forall x) Kx (\exists y)(\exists p) Kyp.$$

The idea of being a thesis of our system is so construed that whenever $\Vdash p$—that is, whenever it is a thesis of our system (**s**) that everyone knows p, so that $\vdash (\forall x) Kxp$—then p itself qualifies as a thesis of our system, so that $\vdash p$. Thus, we have it that $\Vdash p$ entails $\vdash p$ and that $p \Vdash q$ entails $p \vdash q$.

In parallel with the above-mentioned equivalence,
$p \vdash q$ iff $\vdash (p \supset q)$,

we now introduce the coordinate symbolism
$p \Vdash q$ iff $\Vdash (p \supset q)$.

Accordingly, the idea of obvious consequence at issue with $p \Vdash q$ comes to $\vdash (\forall x) Kx(p \supset q)$. In view of the deductivity principle we now also (derivatively) have "If $p \Vdash q$, then $p \vdash q$. Moreover, the following principles will also obtain:
If Kxp and $p \Vdash q$, then Kxq.
If $p \Vdash q$, then $Kxp \vdash Kxq$.

The following $\Vdash$ principles will be stipulated here:
$\Vdash$ *Redundancy*
$\quad p \Vdash p$
$\Vdash$ *Conjunctivity*
$\quad p \,\&\, q \Vdash p$
$\quad p \,\&\, q \Vdash q$
$\Vdash$ *Disjunctivity*
$\quad p \Vdash p \vee q$
$\quad q \Vdash p \vee q$
$\Vdash$ *Veracity*
$\quad Kxp \Vdash p$ and hence also $(\exists x) Kxp \Vdash p$
$\Vdash$ *Contraposition*
$\quad$ If $p \Vdash q$, then $\sim q \Vdash \sim p$.

All of these qualify on essentially logical grounds, and in all of these particular cases the logic of the $\Vdash$-relationship substantially parallels that of the $\vdash$-relationship.

All of these "obvious" inferences are accordingly available to all knowers. The ability to make these several inferences is taken to be part of the defining qualification for counting as a knower, an intelligent being. They are part and parcel of the cognitive availability conception of knowledge that is operative here. To be sure, one could in theory (and perhaps should in practice) credit knowers-in-general with a yet more ample range of "obvious" inferences. But as subsequent deliberations will indicate, these few suffice for an ample development of formative ideas in epistemic logic.

Since $(p \;\&\; q) \Vdash p$, we have it that $\vdash \sim\! Kxp \supset \sim\! Kx(p \;\&\; q)$ for arbitrary q. Thus, once a knower fails to know a fact, the knower fails to "know" a vast number of related facts.

The fact that any two knowers will always know some truths in common means that the realm of truth cannot be divided into two separate hemispheres such that x knows only the truths of one hemisphere while another knower, y, knows only those of the other.

Finite Knower Ignorance

As stated above, the knowers at issue in our discussion are to be imperfect and limited (human) knowers, so that we have $(\forall x)(\exists t)\sim\! Kxt$. Moreover, we cannot but suppose that the ultimately finite history of this finite universe will afford only a finite number of such knowers (very large though it may be). On this basis we can reason as follows: Every knower fails to know *some* truth or other. But now consider the conjunction of all such personally unknown truths for all of the finitely many knowers there are. This monster conjunction of truths will also have to be a truth. But since each knower fails to know some conjunctive constituent within it, nobody knows it as a whole.

Formally developed, the reasoning at issue here can be set out as follows: Let x_i be the i-th member of an inventory of the (inevitably finite) population of knowers: $x_1, x_2, \ldots, x_n$. We can then reason as follows:

1. $(\forall x)(\exists t)\sim\! Kxt$ as above
2. $(\exists t)\sim\! Kx_i t$ from (1)
3. $\sim\! Kx_1 t_i$ for some suitable truth t_i:
                                     from (2) by *existential instantiation*
4. $t^* = t_1 \;\&\; t_2 \;\&\; \ldots \;\&\; t_n$ by definition
5. $\sim\! Kx_i t^*$ from (4) by *veracity* and *conjunctivity*
6. $(\forall x)\sim\! Kxt^*$ from (5)
7. $(\exists t)(\forall x)\sim\! Kxt$ from (6)
8. $\sim\!(\forall t)(\exists x)Kxt$ from (7) QED

Thus, given (1), it follows that $(\forall t)(\exists x) Kxt$ is *not* acceptable. There is a truth of which all finite knowers are ignorant.

And there is another way of looking at the matter as well. Let t^* be the conjunction for all of our (finitely many) knowers of one of their secrets—propositions known to themselves alone.[2] The result will be a true proposition that is known to no individual knower whatsoever. We thus have $\sim (\exists x) Kxt^*$. And in consequence we have it that there will be an unknown truth:

$(\exists t)(\forall x)\sim Kxt$ or equivalently $\sim(\forall t)(\exists x) Kxt$

The idea that every true proposition is known must be abandoned as unacceptable with finite knowers.

In addition to "obvious" (and thus universal) knowledge as per $\Vdash p$ there is also the prospect of "common" knowledge. This comes to $\Vdash (\forall y) Kyp$ or, equivalently, $\vdash (\forall x) Kx(\forall y) Kyp$. Not only is this knowledge that everybody knows, but everybody knows that everybody knows it. Thus, presumably every knower knows not only that "Somebody knows something" or, again, that "Something exists" but also that everybody knows it. However, such knowledge is bound to be of rather limited scope.

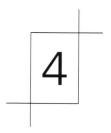

4

Metaknowledge

What Metaknowledge Is All About

Metaknowledge is knowledge about knowledge. Clearly, there will be very different types of metaknowledge. For one thing, such knowledge can be specific and substantive, as in "x knows that y knows that Tokyo is the capital of Japan," or generic and indefinite, as in "Every knower knows that something is known":

$(\forall x)Kx(\exists y)(\exists p)Kyp$

It is, of course, this second mode of purely formal metaknowledge that is at issue here.

The hallmark of metaknowledge is its being a matter of knowing propositions in which one K-operator occurs within the scope of another. Knowledge about someone's ignorance thus counts as metaknowledge. For if x knows of some proposition that y does not know, then we have

$Kx\sim Kyp.$

Examples of such negative metaknowledge are easy to come by. For instance, nobody can know that p is a truth that *nobody* knows:

$(\exists p)Kx(p \,\&\sim(\exists y)Kyp)$

For this would mean (by *conjunctivity*) that x knows p, and this is incompatible with $\sim(\exists y)Kyp$, which also follows. Accordingly,

$$\sim(\exists x)(\exists p)Kx(p \& \sim(\exists y)Kyp)$$

provides a cogent illustration of an item of metaknowledge.

The Knowledge Cooptation Principle

One important item of metaknowledge is that anyone who has knowledge who attributes knowledge to another will have to possess this knowledge himself. We thus have the *knowledge-cooptation principle:*

If $KxKyp$, then Kxp.

This principle follows deductively from principles that have already been stipulated, as follows:

1. Assume $KxKyp$
2. $Kyp \Vdash p$ by *veracity* for $\Vdash$
3. $(\forall x)Kx(Kyp \vdash p)$ from (2) by definition of $\Vdash$
4. $(\forall x)(KxKyp \vdash Kxp)$ from (3) by *deductivity*
5. Kxp from (1), (4) QED

In view of *knowledge cooptation* and *veracity* we will have

$$KxKyp \supset (Kxp \& Kyp).$$

With regard to particular facts, attributed knowledge is shared knowledge. Thus, if x knows of someone that he knows the specific fact p, then x must know this fact as well.

We have not only

If $(\exists y)KxKyp$, then Kxp,

but also

If $Kx(\exists y)Kyp$, then Kxp.

This can be demonstrated as follows:

1. $Kx(\exists y)Kyp$ by hypothesis

2. $(\exists y)Kyp$ from (1) by *veracity*
3. $(\exists y)Kyp \Vdash p$ from $\Vdash$-*veracity* (see the next section)
4. If $Kx(\exists y)Kyp$, then Kxp from (3)
5. Kxp from (2), (4) QED

Knowledge Reflexivity: The *KK* thesis

It is, of course, clear through *veracity* that we have
If $KxKxp$, then Kxp.

But what of the converse of this thesis? Do we automatically have it that knowledge is self-potentiating—that knowers automatically know that they know the following?
If Kxp, then $KxKxp$

This knowledge-reflexivity contention—generally known as the "*KK* thesis"—is something that epistemic logicians have much debated.[1] If it were to obtain as a general thesis, then
$\vdash Kxp \supset KxKxp$.

On this basis we would also have
$\vdash Kxp \supset KxKxKxp$,

and so ever onward. This process of endless self-reflection is clearly problematic for anything like a realistic conception of knowledge. For once we have it that someone (x) knows p, this fact, that Kxp, is available to x by *insight* but surely not by logical inference from the substance of what he knows. For reasons such as these, the *KK* thesis will not be included in the present system. Moreover, there is also a weaker version of knowledge reflexivity based on the thesis that
If Kxp, then $Kx(\exists y)Kyp$.

This thesis asserts that whenever someone knows p, then this individual thereby knows that p is known by *someone*, not necessarily himself. Yet even this is questionable on much the same grounds as before.

To be sure, in envisioning a particularly generous mode of knowledge such as K^*, for which all logico-conceptual ramifications of the known are themselves always credited to a knower, one might be prepared to accept the KK thesis. Thus,

If K^*xp, then K^*xK^*xp

seems to be plausible. But this sort of ampliation is not at issue with the more realistic conception of knowledge that concerns us here.

Secrets

I can certainly know that another individual does not know something that I myself know. There is no problem with

$Ki(p \ \& \sim Kxp)$.

Now, if one person (x) knows something that x knows another person (y) does not know, then x has a secret vis-à-vis y. Here, the situation is

$Kxt \ \& \ Kx\sim Kyt$.

But while knowledge is cooptive—according to $KxKyp \vdash Kxp$—ignorance is not. For if $Kx\sim Kyt$ entailed $\sim Kxt$, then Kxt would entail $\sim Kx\sim Kyt$, and nobody would ever know that something he knows is unknown to another individual. Keeping a secret from someone would become, in principle, impossible.

Accordingly, one can sometimes know that a certain truth known to oneself is not known to any other individual. Knowing

$(\exists t)(Kit \ \& \ Ki\sim(\exists x)[x \neq i \ \& \ Kxt])$

is unproblematic. And in fact the complexity of truth and the diversity of people's access to it means that no two knowers will share the same conjunctive totality of knowledge. (This, of course, does not mean that a knower can never divulge to others some particular limited fact that heretofore has been a secret of his.) This idea that knowers are uniquely characterized by the aggregate of their knowledge can be counted among the fundamental principles of our logic of knowledge.

Epistemic Resolution

A knower comes to an epistemic resolution regarding a proposition p when the knower knows whether p is true or not:

$Kxp \lor Kx{\sim}p$

The limitedness of our knowers means that every knower will be undecided regarding some proposition:

$(\forall x)(\exists p)({\sim}Kxp \ \& \ {\sim}Kx{\sim}p)$

This can be shown as follows. The limitedness of our knowers means that we have

$(\forall x)(\exists t){\sim}Kxt.$

Now, let x be an arbitrary knower. Then by the preceding deliberations we will have it that for some truth t_o it will be the case that ${\sim}Kxt_o$. And, of course, since t_o is a truth, ${\sim}Kx{\sim}t_o$. Accordingly, $(\exists t)({\sim}Kxt \ \& \ {\sim}Kx{\sim}t)$. so that the indicated thesis follows.

As we have seen, no knower x can know that "y knows *that p* is true but I don't":

${\sim}(\exists x)Kx(\exists y)(Kyp \ \& \ {\sim}Kxp)$

This turns out to be self-contradictory. However, there is nothing self-contradictory about the following statement:

$(\exists x)Kx(\exists y)([Kyp \lor Ky{\sim}p] \ \& \ {\sim}Kxp \ \& \ {\sim}Kx{\sim}p)$

A knower x can know perfectly well that "y knows *whether p* is true but I don't."

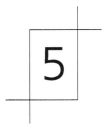

5

For Aught That Someone Knows

A Definition and a Theorem

The idea at issue with "For aught that x knows (to the contrary), p is the case" is captured by the definition

Axp iff $\sim(\exists q)(Kxq\ \&\ Kx[q \vdash \sim p])$.

On this basis it becomes possible to establish that if p obtains for aught that x knows, then x does not know not-p.[1]

$Axp \vdash \sim Kx\sim p$

This can be shown as follows:

1. Axp	assumption
2. $\sim(\exists q)(Kxq\ \&\ Kx[q \vdash \sim p])$	from (1) by definition A
3. $(\forall q)\ (\sim Kxq \vee \sim Kx[q \vdash \sim p])$	from (2)
4. $\sim Kx\sim p \vee \sim Kx[\sim p \vdash \sim p])$	from (3) substituting $\sim p/q$
5. $\sim Kx\sim p$	from (4) and $\sim p \Vdash \sim p$

And it is also possible to establish the converse of this theorem:

$\sim Kx\sim p \vdash Axp$ or equivalently $\sim Axp \vdash Kx\sim p$

For by the definition of *Axp* this amounts to
$$(\exists q)(Kxq \;\&\; Kx[q \vdash \sim p]) \vdash Kx\sim p.$$

And this follows at once from the thesis at hand by the *deductivity principle*.

Accordingly, we have it that
Axp iff $\sim Kx\sim p$.

This equivalence affords an alternative and compact way of specifying the idea that "For aught that *x* knows to the contrary, *p* is the case," namely, "*x* does not know that not-*p*." Notwithstanding any seeming difference, these two contentions are demonstrably equivalent. Note that *Axp* and *Ax*~*p* are perfectly compatible, seeing that one can be totally in the dark regarding *p*'s truth status.

The Bearing of Veracity

The principle of *veracity* entails that $(\forall x)(\forall t)\sim Kx\sim t$ or equivalently $(\forall x)(\forall t)Axt$. For consider:

1. $Kxp \supset p$ — *veracity*
2. $\sim p \supset \sim Kxp$ — from (1) by contraposition
3. $p \supset \sim Kx\sim p$ — from (2) by substituting $\sim p/p$
4. $(\forall x)(\forall t)Axt$ — from (3) QED

In summary, any truth is true for aught that anybody knows. What anyone actually knows is always compatible with the truth at large—and thereby also with the knowledge of others. Knowledge at large is comprehensively coherent.

It has already been noted in chapter 1 that
$$\sim(\exists x)(\exists p)Kx(p \;\&\; \sim(\exists y)Kyp).$$

This is equivalent with
$$(\forall x)(\forall p)\sim Kx\sim(p \supset (\exists y)Kyp).$$

Observe, however, that this is something quite different from
$(\forall x) \sim Kx \sim (\forall p)(p \supset (\exists y) Kyp)$ or equivalently $(\forall x) Ax (\forall t)(\exists y) Kyt$.

This thesis claims that for aught that anyone knows, every truth is actually known by someone. And this contention is quite incorrect. For suppose a coin is tossed onto a superheated surface where it is instantly vaporized. It must be a truth either that it landed heads or that it landed tails. But in the circumstance it is not possible for anyone to know which is the case. So there will be a truth that no one knows and no one can possibly know. (Subsequent discussions below will confront us with other such unknowables.)

We do, however, have it that if x knows that p is unknown—that nobody knows p—then for aught that x knows, p is false:

If $Kx \sim (\exists y) Kyp$, then $Ax \sim p$

This can be shown as follows:

1. $Kx \sim (\exists y) Kyp$	by supposition
2. $\sim (\exists y) Kyp$	(1) by veracity
3. $\sim Kxp$	from (2)
4. $\sim Kx \sim \sim p$	from (3)
5. $Ax \sim p$	from (4)

However, consider

If $Kx \sim (\exists y) Kyp$, then Axp,

or, equivalently,

if $Kx \sim p$, then $\sim Kx \sim (\exists y) Kyp$.

Clearly, if $Kx \sim p$, then $\sim p$, and therefore $\sim (\exists y) Kyp$. In these evidences it is perfectly plausible that x should know that $\sim (\exists y) Kyp$ obtain so that $Kx \sim (\exists y) Kyp$. The implication in question thus fails to hold.

Ignorance

The idea that x is in the dark about p—does not "have a clue" as to whether p or $\sim p$—is conveyed by $\sim Kxp$ & $\sim Kx \sim p$ or equivalently Axp & $Ax\sim p$. And the principle of *knower limitedness* assures that

$$(\forall x)(\exists p)(Axp \ \& \ Ax\sim p).$$

This can be established as follows:

1.	$(\exists p)(p \ \& \sim Kxp)$	*knower limitedness*
2.	$(\forall p)(p \supset \sim(\exists x)Kx\sim p)$	by *veracity*
3.	$(\exists p)(\sim Kx\sim p \ \& \sim Kxp)$	from (1), (2)
4.	$(\exists p)(\sim Kx\sim p \ \& \sim Kx\sim\sim p)$	from (3)
5.	$(\forall x)(\exists p)(Axp \ \& \ Ax\sim p)$	from (4)

Every (limited) knower is accordingly in the dark about something. This means that while the truth and knowledge are consistent, the manifold of propositions that are true for aught that someone knows is not. (Both p and $\sim p$ can belong to it.)

Since no one among our *ex hypothesi* limited knowers is omniscient, it follows that $(\forall t)Kxt$ is flat-out false. This being so, no one knows it to be true.

$$\sim(\exists x)Kx(\forall t)Kxt$$

And this comes to

$$(\forall x)\sim Kx\sim(\exists t)\sim Kxt \text{ or equivalently } (\forall x)Ax(\exists t)\sim Kxt.$$

For aught that anyone knows, there is some truth they themselves do not know.

The idea that x is ignorant regarding p—that p is true but x does not know it—is conveyed by the definition

$$x \text{ ig } p \text{ iff } p \ \& \sim Kxp.$$

This leads straightaway to the equivalence

$$x \text{ ig } p \text{ iff } p \ \& \ Ax\sim p.$$

Accordingly, x is ignorant regarding p if p is in fact true, and yet for aught that x knows, not-p obtains. The finding of the preceding paragraph means that

$$(\forall x)Ax(\exists p)x \text{ ig } p.$$

Cognitive Indeterminacy

A cognitively undetermined proposition is one of which no one knows whether it is true or not:

undet(p) iff $\sim(\exists x)Kxp$ & $\sim(\exists y)Ky\sim p$

This comes to

$(\forall x)Axp$ & $(\forall x)Ax\sim p$.

That is, for aught that anyone knows an undetermined proposition is true but also for aught that anyone knows so is its negation: nobody knows about its truth status one way or the other.

The thesis that there are such propositions comes to

$(\exists p)(\sim(\exists x)Kxp$ & $\sim(\exists y)Ky\sim p)$.

or equivalently

$\sim(\forall p)((\exists x)Kxp \vee (\exists y)Ky\sim p)$.

Now, consider the negation of this claim, $(\forall p)((\exists x)Kxp \vee (\exists y)Ky\sim p)$, which effectively asserts that every proposition is either known (by someone) to be true or known (by someone) to be false. Now if this were the case and held for *all* propositions, then it would be true for all *true* ones, with the consequence that all truths are known, $(\forall t)(\exists x)Kxt$. Since this consequence is clearly untenable, the existence of cognitively undetermined propositions must be accepted. The ramifications of this fact will be considered in greater detail in chapter 9.

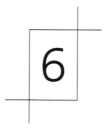

6

Group Knowledge

Individuals versus Groups

A great deal of knowledge is not individual and personal but collective and social, the "knower" at issue being a group rather than an individual. And it is by no means easy to describe how group knowledge is related to individual knowledge. From the epistemic standpoint a team of individuals, say $\{x, y\}$, consisting of x and y, has to be treated as a new, different entity in its own right. Such a collectivity will know things that no individual does—and this not only in the sense of performatory "know-how" but in factual matters as well. With large physics experiments, for example, it is the engineers rather than the theorists who understand the workings of the equipment used for experimentation and the theorists rather than the engineers who understand the significance of the results. Such complications bring new issues to light because the situation that obtains in the logic of knowledge changes substantially with the shift from individual to group knowers.

Suppose that two individuals are being asked about the array of six letters and that their knowledge of the matter is as follows:

x: A _ A _ A _
y: _ B _ B _ B

Neither individual has a clue that another letter is at issue, different from the one he happens to know about. And neither has an inkling that what is at issue is a trio of AB pairs: ABABAB. As this example illustrates, no one can foresee what will arise when an individual's own information is pooled with or supplemented by that of others. So no one is in a position to say anything definitive about what a collaborative "team" consisting of members bringing different sorts of expertise to bear will collectively know, other than that it will encompass all of the knowledge they themselves possess: If Kxp, then $K\{x, y\}p$.

Group Knowledge and Knowledge Pooling

It is commonplace to speak of collective knowledge and say things like "We nowadays know that the sun is a thermonuclear reactor and not just a large fire" or "In the twentieth century people knew a great deal more about Antarctica than they did in the days of Captain Cook." How is one to interpret such locutions?

There are several importantly different senses of group knowledge. To begin with, one must distinguish between the distributive sense, K_d, and the collective sense, K_c, of knowledge:

1. A group knows something *distributively* whenever some member of the group knows this fact. Thus,

$K_d Gp$ iff $(\exists x)(x \in G \ \& \ Kxp)$.

An item of information is accordingly known to a group in this distributive sense just in case it is known to someone in the group.

2. A group knows something *collectively* if every member of the group knows this fact. Thus,

$K_c Gp$ iff $(\forall x)(x \in G \supset Kxp)$.

This, of course, is a very restricted sort of group knowledge, confirming its range to what is universally recognized.

Yet another sense of the term must also be considered:

3. A group knows something *aggregatively* if this fact can be derived from the totality of what the group members individually know:

$K_a Gp$ iff $(\exists p_1)(\exists p_2) \ldots (\exists p_n)(\exists x_1 \in G)(\exists x_2 \in G) \ldots (\exists x_n \in G)$
$(Kx_1 p_1, \ \& \ Kx_2 p_2, \ \& \ Kx_n p_n, \ \& \ \ldots (p_1 \ \& \ p_2 \ \& \ldots \ \& \ p_n \vdash p))$

An item of information is accordingly known to a group in this collective sense if it is inferentially available from what the group members know individually. The peculiarity here is that no single group member may actually know the item at issue (in even the most liberal sense of the term).

Finally, there is also yet another more realistic sense of group knowledge that functions more loosely but also more usefully than any of the preceding.

4. A group knows something by way of *expert knowledge* if this is known to the general run of its experts:

$K_e Gp$ iff p is accepted by some (or most) of those group members who are best informed on the relevant issues.

It is usually this sense of the term that comes closest to what people have in mind when speaking of group knowledge in the manner of "What the Greeks already know" or of "What is known nowadays."

These four senses of group knowledge are substantially different, and each is subject to its own characteristic logical principles. For example, if x knows p (but not q) and y knows q (but not p), then we will *not* have $K_d\{x, y\}(p \& q)$. However, we will have $K_a\{x, y\}(p \& q)$, since $p \& q$ can readily be inferred when the knowledge of x and of y are pooled. When a group knows something in the aggregative accessibility sense, then there may be no single group member who knows this fact. So by construing group knowledge in *this* sense we arrive at something rather—and perhaps overly—remote from our common understanding of the matter.

There is little doubt, however, that how people generally conceive of group knowledge is something that has changed over time. Prior to the seventeenth century the idea of experiential knowledge focused (under Aristotle's influence) on what we humans all know from common experience—pretty much as per $K_e Gp$ with G as people at large. However, as the idea of a scientific community came to the fore, there came a shift to the more diffuse and multilateral sort of expert knowledge based on the experiment-based experience of scientific experts.

Collective Ignorance

It is readily established that if x is ignorant about the truth status of p and y is ignorant about the truth status of q, then there is a truth functional combination of p and q about which both x and y are ignorant. For when this is the case, then the conjunction of p or $\sim p$ (whatever is true) with q or not-q (whatever is true) will be unknown alike to both x and y, irrespective of what else it is that they do or do not know. And this generalizes in such a way that if *each* member of a finite group of knowers G is against what the truth status of some proposition or other is, then there is some single collective proposition about whose truth status *all* G-members will be ignorant. We thus have

If $(\forall x \in G)(\exists p)x\ ig\ p$, then $(\exists p)(\forall x \in G)\ x\ ig\ p$,

where $x\ ig\ p$ iff $\sim Kxp\ \&\ \sim Kx\sim p$.

Distributive versus Collective Cooperation in Knowledge Development

There are two very different modes of multilaterally cooperative investigation, since a multiparticipant problem-solving effort can proceed either collectively or distributively. *Distributive cooperation* is simply a matter of those concerned making a separate effort toward the realization of a shared goal, whereas actual *collaboration* or *collective cooperation* is a matter of teamwork, of those concerned working together toward a goal with interactive feedback. (The term *cooperation* accordingly serves as a broader umbrella to cover both of these cases.)

Distributive problem solving occurs when the issues are disassembled into separate components that are addressed separately—often by distinct investigators—subject to a division of labor. Perhaps because variant specialties are at issue, each investigator (or investigative group) works separately and individually, and their combined efforts, though coordinated, are disjoint, with different participants contributing different pieces of the whole. Thus, with the lexicographic problem of explaining the etymology of English words we may have a research mode where investigator 1 may take on the A's, investigator 2 the B's, and so on. Again, in a cryptological effort one investigator might work on verbs and adverbs, another on nouns and adjectives, and another on particles. That is, different investigators take on different constituent subproblems of the whole, like subcontractors contributing their separate operations to an overall effort.

However, a very different situation emerges when cooperative problem solving proceeds collaboratively. Here, there is not just cooperation but actual *teamwork,* with different investigators fusing their efforts in conjoint interaction. Collaborative work on a crossword puzzle is a good example. As anyone who has tried it knows, collaborating on a puzzle brings into play a feedback interaction that produces something far more effective than what would be achieved if the results of different individuals working separately were simply compiled. For problem solving then proceeds interactively, with the efforts of the different contributors inextricably interwoven. And we shall suppose that with genuinely collaborative cooperation none of the individuals involved is dispensable in that the work of the others would not yield the discovery at issue without this individual's contribution.[1]

There are, of course, some problems that cannot be factored into constituent pieces. Such systemic problems as, for example, explaining the origins of World War I must be handled as an indivisible unit: To achieve unified causal account it makes no sense to address the historical, political, colonial, social, military, naval, and economic aspects of the problem in separation. By their very nature as such, these are holistic problems where multilateral cooperation must of necessity take the form of interactive teamwork.[2] However, irrespective of the mode of cooperation, the key fact remains that the knowledge available to a collaborating team will be substantially greater than the mere conjoining or compilation of the knowledge of its individual members.

In view of this book's focus on *individual* knowledge, the topic of group knowledge will not be pursued much further. This focus is a matter of division of labor and must not be construed as denying the importance of the topic.

Propositional versus Interrogative Knowledge

That Knowledge versus *What* Knowledge

From a logical standpoint there is a significant difference between knowing *that* and knowing *what*, between *propositional* and non-propositionally *interrogative* knowledge. For one can represent "*x* knows that *p*"—say, that the cat is sitting on the mat—by an expression of the format *Kxp*, where *p* is a complete proposition. But more complex machinery is required for saying that "*x* knows *what* the cat is doing"—and, similarly, with other interrogative pronouns such as *who, where, when, why,* and *how*. For, here, one will have to deal not simply with *propositions* but with *propositional functions,* and quantifying over them becomes necessary.

Observe, to begin with, that we can generally represent interrogative, question-geared knowledge in terms of propositional that-qualified knowledge by the expedient of a conjunction to the effect that

1. there is some answer to that interrogative what-who-where-style question, and
2. *x* knows it. (Note here the *it*-referenced anaphoric back-reference to item 1.)

The situation is illustrated by rendering "x knows where the treasure is buried" as

$(\exists p)(p$ correctly answers the question Q of where the treasure is buried & $Kx[p$ answers $Q])$.

Or, again, "x knows who buried the treasure" can be rendered as

$(\exists p)(p$ correctly answers the question Q of where the treasure is buried & $Kx[p$ answers $Q])$.

Thus, the common format for all such renditions will be

$(\exists p)(p @ Q \,\&\, Kx(p @ Q))$

Here, $p @ Q$ abbreviates "p answers Q (correctly and appropriately)" or "p is a correct and appropriate answer to Q." Since knowledge must be veridical, the previous thesis can be restated less redundantly:

$(\exists p)Kx(p @ Q)$

This symbolic statement asserts that "x knows the answer to Q," and it is the explicit involvement of a suitable question that leads to the designation of "interrogative knowledge" for these cases.

Note here the absence of any claim that *we*, those who make this assertion, know specifically what that answer is. Moreover, it should further be observed that the cognate (standardly propositional) thesis

$Kx(\exists p)[p @ Q]$

will not do the job at all. It claims only that x knows *that* there is an answer to our question but not that x knows *what* that answer is. To make *this* claim we must quantify into the substantive content of our knower's knowledge. And this leads to further complications.

To represent interrogative knowledge adequately it will not do simply to prefix our knowledge operator Kx to some self-contained proposition. Instead, it now becomes necessary to reach into a K-governed context *from without*.[1] For now we are not attributing knowledge of something to an individual but merely dealing with the indefinitely quantified fact:

There is some proposition or other that meets a certain condition and the knower at issue knows this proposition.

We must thus indicate the substance of the knowledge at issue in the object-geared *de re* mode, and not just assert *de dicto* some known fact. Accordingly—and this is the key point—all such interrogative knowledge fails to exhibit the standard format that an individual knows some definitively specified proposition. For here the proposition at issue is never definitely stated. Indeed, we, the assertors, may well not be able to say what it specifically is. As far as we are concerned, the substance of our knower's knowledge is treated at arm's length.

It is for just this reason that knowledge about one's own ignorance must be framed interrogatively. One cannot say "You know that *p*, but I don't" or "You know that someone knows *p*, but I don't," though one can perfectly well say "You know whether *p* or not, but I don't" or "Somebody knows whether *p* is true or not, but I don't."

Answering and Identification

"What is the sum of two plus two?" Consider the following range of responses: four, two times two, two squared, the smallest nonprime number, the second largest square number, the number of George Brown's siblings. None of these is exactly wrong, yet only the first qualifies as the unproblematically correct and appropriate *direct answer* to our question. The question is effectively short for "What *number*, in the manner that numbers are standardly indicated, is the sum of two plus two?" And only the first answer precludes this issue from arising again as per "What number is two times two?" and so on.

Again, consider the question "Who is the eldest son of the philosopher Moses Mendelssohn?" The feasible responses include all three of the following: Abraham Mendelssohn, the father of Felix Mendelssohn Bartholdy, the male parent of the composer of the well-known "A Midsummer Night's Dream." But it is only the first direct rather than indirect answer that is appropriate. For our question was effectively short for "What is the name of the eldest son of Moses Mendelssohn?" And only the first answer brings matters to a conclusion here. In asking for something to be identified we require a standardized, type-canonical identification (with numbers their value, with people their name). We want a *direct* answer, one that is presented in the standard way and not just some roundabout indication of the item at issue as satisfying some elaborate albeit pertinent description or other that leaves the matters of an informative identification still unresolved. Identifying differs from individuating: it looks to a standardized mode of specification.

Consider the following exchange:

A: "I know who committed the murder."

B: "Really! Who?"

A: "The man whose footprint is in the flower-bed over there."

Here *A*'s response, however true, fails to do the job. Knowing whom is more demanding than that. For while *A* is able to *individuate* the individual at issue—that is, to specify a property or feature that this individual alone has—*A* does not qualify as being able to *identify* that individual. Yes, *A* does have *an* answer to the question "Who committed the murder?" that is, "The man whose footprint is in the flower bed over there." But this answer has not met the demands of an authentically direct identification. It is one thing to offer a true response to a question, but something else—and more—actually to answer it directly. Without identification, *x* does not have an informatively *appropriate* answer. The crucial difference here is between the actual identification of an item and its mere individuating specification by some description that is unique to it. Thus "Don Juan, the famous rake" identifies the individual but "the man—whoever he is—who fathered yon child" does not. For although this response is *individuating*, it does not *identify* the person at issue and so would not count as successfully answering the question "Whom did Pedro the Cruel most notably imprison for licentiousness?"

The point is that there are standard and canonical ways of identifying objects of a particular type—people by name, numbers by quantity, and so on—and that unless one is able to specify an item in the canonical way one does not really qualify as being able to identify it. Accordingly, for maintaining that "x knows whom Wellington defeated at Waterloo" we would require that x realizes that it was *Napoleon* who was defeated there and not just "the victor of the Battle of Austerlitz" or "the losing commander at the Battle of Borodino."

So when we look to the truth conditions of a thesis of the format $KxFu$,

we must include among them that x be in a position to specify the item at issue in a manner that F relevantly *identifies* it in the standard, type-canonical way at issue with F. Thus, the claim that "x knows where the Eiffel Tower is located" will be in order if x knows that the Eiffel Tower is in Paris, but not if x only knows, say, that it is in the city where Marat was assassinated. For although it is not false to place the Eiffel Tower there, it is sufficiently off the mark that it could not qualify as a direct or appropriate answer. After all, the claim that x knows a certain fact is here made on *our* account: when we say that x knows the "Eiffel Tower is in Paris" then means that the Eiffel Tower at issue and the Paris at issue are those items as *we* think of them. If all that x is convinced of is that "The principal structure erected by the Eiffel Company during 1887–1889 is located in the French city besieged by the Germans for over a month in 1870," then one would not begin to do justice to the situation by saying that "x knows the Eiffel Tower is in Paris." Such a claim would be inappropriate and incorrect.

Substituting Equivalents in Epistemic Contexts

The preceding deliberations indicate that with $KxFu$ it is x—and not we ourselves—who is in charge of the knowledge situation regarding F. So even if F and G are demonstrably equivalent as per $\vdash (Fu \equiv Gu)$, we nevertheless cannot make an interchange when $KxFu$ and go to, say, $KxGu$. For while the equivalence in question is part of fact

and of *our* knowledge of fact, it may well nevertheless not be a part of
x's knowledge. For that interchange to be appropriate we would have
to be operating within the orbit of x's knowledge—that is, we would
need to have $Kx(\vdash Fu \equiv Gu)$. Analogously, even if Kxp and $\vdash (p \equiv q)$,
we cannot automatically infer Kxq but would require $Kx \vdash (p \equiv q)$.
And the same proviso holds good for the move from $Kx(\exists p)F(p)$ to
$Kx(\exists p)G(p)$.

   Accordingly, it will not in general be the case that
   If $Kx(Qu)Fu$ and $Fu \vdash Gu$, then $Kx(Qu)Gu$, where Q is one of our
   quantifiers $\forall$ and $\exists$.

Since here u first occurs *after* the knowledge prefix Kx, it is x who is in
charge of the cognitive situation and whose state of knowledge regarding implicative relationships is determinative.[2] However, the case
is quite different with the inference
   If $(Qu)KxFu$ and $Fu \vdash Gu$, then $(Qu)KxGu$.

This represents a perfectly cogent mode of reasoning because that initial, out-front quantifier puts us in charge of what is being said.

   For the sake of illustration, consider the following situation:
   $Su = u$ is one of the following F-A-M-L-T states: Florida, Alaba-
   ma, Mississippi, Louisiana, Texas.
   $Gu = u$ is a Gulf state.
   $Cu = u$ was part of the Confederacy.

Now let it be that $(Kx)(\forall u)(Gu \supset Cu)$ or "x knows that the Gulf states
were part of the Confederacy." Since by the definition of "Gulf state"
we have $\vdash \forall u(Su \equiv Gu)$, it follows that $(Su \supset Cu)$. But this is something that *we* are presumed to know by virtue of our use of that expression. But x cannot be presumed to know it. So $Kx(\forall u)(Su \supset Gu)$
or "x knows that F-A-M-L-T were part of the Confederacy" need not
be the case, since x may well not realize the F-A-M-L-T states are the
Gulf states. On the other hand, $(\forall u)Kx(Gu \supset Cu)$ or "x knows of each
of the F-A-M-L-T states that it was a member of the Confederacy" will
indeed follow from that initial assertion. This is so because it is we our-

selves, those of us who realize that $Su \vdash Gu$, who are in charge of defining the group at issue in our knowledge attribution to x.

And therefore we have the inferential rule: When an initial quantifier stands in front of a knowledge prefix, then—but only then!—is one free to carry on deductive inferences with the so quantified propositional function that stands behind it.

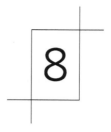

8

Collective versus Distributive Knowledge and Knower Limitedness

Collective and Distributive Characterizations

Let S be a set of objects or items of some sort. Then an individual x has *collective* (or composite, *in sensu composito*) knowledge that S-members have a certain feature F when

$$Kx(\forall u)(u \in S \supset Fu).$$

Here, x knows that whatever belongs to S will have the feature F and thereby knows a certain general fact regarding S-membership at large, namely, that it involves only F-possessors.

By contrast, x knows *distributively* (or *in sensu diviso*) of each and every object that if it is an S-member then it has F:

$$(\forall u)Kx(u \in S \supset Fu)$$

Note that in both cases x must have the concept of S-membership, but in neither case need x know what particular individuals belong to S[1]; x's knowledge of S must be intensional, but not necessarily extensional.

Even when the range of the objects of knowledge is finite *and known*, there nevertheless remains significant difference between the collective and distributive knowledge of the preceding distinction. For suppose that this range is simply the set $\{a, b, c\}$. Then $(\forall u)KxFu$ comes to $KxFa$ & $KxFb$ & $KxFc$ or equivalently $Kx(Fa$ & Fb & $Fc)$ by the principle of conjunctivity. However, $Kx(\forall u)Fu$ requires not just $KxFa$ & $KxFb$ & $KxFc$ (which is equivalent to the preceding) but also knowledge that the $\forall$-range includes (only) a and b and c. For now that universal quantifier functions *within* the range of x's knowledge.

Thus, in dealing with an imponderable manifold—such as "lions" or "knowers"—whose open-ended membership we could not even begin to inventory, it will only be collective knowledge that can ever be accessible to us. For example, unless x is inordinately dense, x will realize that everything is self-identical: $Kx(\forall u)(u = u)$. But we nevertheless cannot maintain that x actually knows of everything that is self-identical: $(\forall u)Kx(u = u)$. For if x is not even aware of some u_0's existence, we certainly cannot maintain that x is aware of *its* self-identity (note here that anaphoric back reference to u_0 in specific which, by hypothesis, lies outside the horizon of x's ken.) The distinctions at issue here carry over from universal to particular knowledge. Thus, x knows in generic abstractness that some S's have a certain feature F whenever

$$Kx(\exists u)(u \in S \,\&\, Fu).$$

By contrast, x knows concretely (specifically) of certain particular S's that they have a feature F whenever

$$(\exists u)Kx(u \in S \,\&\, Fu).$$

Here, x knows not only that some S has F but also which one.[2]

The crux of the difference between collectively generic and concretely specific knowledge lies in the issue of "quantifying-in," that is, of the sequencing of the quantifier at issue ($\mathbf{Q}$) and the knowledge operator K by way of $K\mathbf{Q}$ or $\mathbf{Q}K$. The logical difference at issue is significant because distributive knowledge once again requires quantifying into K-contexts so that the knower bears the referential responsibility. To say that x knows distributively that F characterizes all the individuals at issue comes to

$$(\forall u)KxFu.$$

And here it is crucial that the quantifier reaches into the K-context and controls it from without, unlike

$$Kx(\forall u)Fu,$$

which says that x knows that F is a universal property, applicable to everything.

There is no problem with "For every u, x knows that Fu" in the sense of $Kx(\forall u)Fu$, namely, that x knows that every u F's. However, "For every u, x knows that it F's in the sense of $(\forall u)KxFu$ is something else again. Thus, while we know that "Every (or any) even number is divisible by two" because all of them are, one does not know *of* every (any, all) even number that it *is* divisible by two. For that anaphoric back-reference to an "it" requires a pre-identified item, and this sort of thing is not practicable when finite knowers are addressing an infinite set of objects.[3]

This distinction makes a very substantial difference. There can be little doubt about the capacity of finite knowers to know universal truths: "x knows that all humans are mortal" is an unproblematic instance of knowing a collective fact. But the corresponding distributive case is something else again. Maintaining that "x knows of every human that he or she is mortal" is simply not practicable with finite knowers, seeing that there is simply no possible way for such a knower x to get around to considering all the relevant instances.

Aspects of Knower Limitedness

The knowers that are at issue in our present deliberations are not only *finite* but also *limited* knowers. They are emphatically not omniscient and their knowledge is incomplete and imperfect. Here we have the thesis of *knower limitedness:*

> The knowledge of each knower is incomplete; for each knower there is some truth that this individual does not know:
>
> $(\forall x)(\exists t)\sim Kxt$ or equivalently $\sim(\exists x)(\forall t)Kxt$[4]

So every knower within our purview is cognitively imperfect. For any and every x, we have it that, "There is a truth that x does not—and, indeed, as will soon emerge, *cannot*—know." But just what can one know about this ignorance of ours? Since for every limited knower x there is some truth that x does not know, it transpires that when there are but finitely many knowers, there will be a truth—to wit, the conjunction of the individual unknowns for all the various knowers—that none of them knows. There can thus be no question about the tenability of

$(\exists t)(\forall x) \sim Kxt$.

Self-Awareness of Limitation

Since "I know it to be the case both that p and that I don't know that p" symbolically $Ki(p \ \& \sim Kip)$ is self-contradictory—as we have seen—it transpires that nobody ever knows that a proposition they do not know is nevertheless true:

$\sim(\exists x)(\exists p)Kx(p \ \& \sim Kxp)$ or equivalently $(\forall x)(\forall p)\sim Kx(p \ \&$
$\sim Kxp)$

Interestingly, this inescapable contention is logically equivalent with $(\forall x)(\forall p)\sim Kx\sim(p \supset Kxp)$ or equivalently $(\forall x)(\forall p)Kx(p \supset Kxp)$.

This, of course, implies $(\forall p)Ki(p \supset Kip)$. For aught that anyone knows, when a particular proposition is true, they themselves know it. (And this holds true despite the fact that finite knowers know perfectly well that they do not know everything, $Ki\sim(\forall p)(p \supset Kip)$. Here, again, the order of K and $\forall$ makes a big difference.

Membership in the realm of by-oneself-unknown truth is something that lies outside one's cognitive ken. Nobody knows that they do not know a *particular* truth.[5] And this, of course, means that our knowledge about our ignorance is going to be distinctly limited. I certainly know that there are truths I do not know: $Ki(\exists p)(p \ \& \sim Kip)$. But I do not—cannot—know of some truth t that I do not know it, $\sim(\exists p)Ki(p \ \& \sim Kip)$, since the negation of this contention is clearly self-contradictory. While I know *that* there are facts that I do not know, I cannot know *what* these facts are. Our ignorance is hidden away in a cognitive blind spot: we do not—cannot—know the specific substance of our ignorance.[6]

As these deliberations have repeatedly stressed, the identification of unknowable truths is in principle impossible, so that the extent to which we can be specific regarding our ignorance is limited. Consider the sequence of these statements:

I do not know anything about Nepal.

I do not know what the capital of Nepal is.

I do not know that Katmandu is the capital of Nepal.

There is no problem with the first two statements. But the third—at least in its natural construal as "Katmandu is the capital of Nepal and I do not know it"—is simply paradoxical.

We can, do, and must suppose that all (finite) knowers know of their own cognitive limitedness and accordingly envision a universal recognition of cognitive imperfection. Thus, we have

$$\Vdash (\forall x)(\exists t) \sim Kxt$$

and, accordingly,

$$(\forall y)Ky(\forall x)(\exists t) \sim Kxt.$$

Setting $x = y$, this straightaway yields

$$(\forall y)Ky(\exists t) \sim Kyt.$$

This, too, is an aspect of the universal self-recognition of cognitive limitedness.

The preceding section noted that for any x

$$(\forall p) \sim Kx(p \ \& \sim Kxp) \text{ or equivalently } \sim(\exists p)Kx(p \ \& \sim Kxp).$$

Moreover, we have just seen that for any finite knower x

$$Kx(\exists p)(p \ \& \sim Kxp).$$

Now, this combination of theses of types

$$Kx(\exists p)F(x, p) \text{ and } \sim(\exists p)KxF(x, p)$$

is significant. It puts us into the characteristic situation of noninstantiability: of knowing that there exist items having a certain feature but not being able to adduce a single instance that possesses this feature.

(The feature at issue in this case is that of being a truth not known to *x*—for example, oneself.)

And this means, most importantly, that we cannot possibly know the *extent* of our ignorance. For while we can indeed know that there are questions we cannot answer, we cannot see our way through to those further questions that lie beyond our cognitive horizon. By knowing the overall size of the earth, the cartographers of the seventeenth century could determine the extent of terra incognita. But not knowing the size of the cognitive realm, we can make no comparable assessment of the magnitude of cognitive terra incognita. Here in this cognitive context—unlike the geographic one—we cannot possibly assess the extent of a domain of items we cannot specifically identify.[7]

A Key Limitation

Future contingencies afford plausible-seeming examples of unknowns. For who among us can possibly say who will be elected U.S. president in the year 2400? Also, it is well known that there are mathematical sentences that can neither be demonstrated nor refuted; we will have

$(\exists p)(\sim(\exists x)Kxp \,\&\, \sim(\exists x)Kx\sim p).$

And since either *p* or alternatively not-*p* must inevitably be true, it follows that

$(\exists t)\sim(\exists x)Kxt$ or equivalently $(\exists t)(\forall x)\sim Kxt$ or equivalently $\sim(\forall t)(\exists x)Kxt.$

There are truths that, for aught that anyone actually knows, are not truths. Our knowledge of the truth is unavoidably deficient, for with limited knowers there must be unknown truths:

$(\exists t)\sim(\exists y)Kyt$ or equivalently $(\exists t)(\forall y)\sim Kyt$ or again $\sim(\forall t)$
$(\exists y)Kyt$

After all, the endless (syntactic) complexity of propositions—including some true ones—puts some of them outside the scope of what finite intelligences can conceive. Since no knower can "think" these truths, it follows that no one can *know* them either.

As indicated, we certainly know that unknowns exist:

$(\exists t)(\forall x) \sim Kxt.$

Nevertheless, nobody knows of any particular (true) proposition that it is altogether unknown. For while such ignorance may very well obtain in some case, no one can actually *know* it. After all, $Kx(p \ \& \sim(\exists y)Kyp)$ is self-contradictory, as we have seen. And this being so, our system **s** cannot for any specific proposition p whatsoever assert that

$\vdash (p \ \& \sim(\exists x)Kxp),$

since this would straightaway lead to a self-contradiction.

However, there is no problem with a *conjecture* to the effect that p is a truth that nobody knows. Thus,

$* (p \ \& \sim(\exists x)Kxp)$

is in principle a perfectly tenable assertion. For while both $*p$ and $*\sim(\exists x)Kxp$ follow from this, there will be no contradiction here. "I surmise that Katmandu is the capital of Nepal, though I do not actually know it" is a perfectly viable locution. Reasonable conjectures about our ignorance will be possible even where knowledge of it is not.

To be sure, in dealing with the limits of knowledge, we are not so much interested in what people *do not* know as in what they *cannot* know; our concern is not with our limitations but with our limits—with *inevitable* ignorance. This issue of truths that knowers cannot know lies at the heart of the subsequent deliberations, and its concern for what is possible and what is not leads next to the topic of modality.

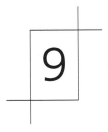

9

Modality

How Modality Works: Possibility and Necessity

Let us now consider quantified modal logic (QML) in an epistemic perspective. The logical modalities of possibility ($\Diamond$) and necessity ($\Box$) that function in this domain are subject to the following principles:

If $\Box p$, then p.
If p, then $\Diamond p$.

Moreover, they are also subject to the *principles of modal duality*:

$\Diamond p$ iff $\sim\Box\sim p$.
$\Box p$ iff $\sim\Diamond\sim p$.

The validation of necessity claims inheres in exploring logico-conceptual relationships. In particular, when p is demonstrable, then it is thereby demonstrably necessary:

If $\vdash p$, then $\Box p$, and indeed $\vdash \Box p$.

This, however, is less a fact about necessity as such than an artifact of the policy of asserting in our system only those theses adjudged to be necessary in the specific mode of *epistemic* necessity that cashes in on the particular idea of knowledge that is to be at issue.

The necessity operator is subject to the logical principle

If $\Box(p \supset q)$, then $\Box p \supset \Box q$.

Necessary implication yields corresponding implications between necessities. And this principle in turn yields

If $\Box(p \supset q)$, then $\Diamond p \supset \Diamond q$.

Quantification with respect to individuals, be it universal ($\forall$) or existential ($\exists$), interacts with modality as follows:

$\Box(\forall u)Fu \vdash (\forall u)\Box Fu$

$(\exists u)\Diamond Fu \vdash \Diamond(\exists u)Fu$

The second of these obtains because if some actual individual possibly F's, then there is a coherent scenario—a story, if you will, in which this individual actually F's. And the first thesis is a logical consequence of the second, thanks to the generality of F.[1]

When a modal operator ($\Diamond$ or $\Box$) stands before a *complete proposition*, we have an instance of modality *de dicto* (statement modality). But when modality applies to a propositional function that is subject to external quantification, we have an instance of *de re* (object modality) with respect to the items at issue. And so the two just-indicated relationships show that

with universal statements, *de dicto* implies *de re* necessity; and

with existential statements, *de re* implies *de dicto* possibility.

These two principles are basic to quantified modal logic.[2]

While $(\exists u)\Diamond Fu$ entails $\Diamond(\exists u)Fu$, the two are very different in meaning. The former asserts, "There is some actual object that might have F," whereas the latter asserts, "It is possible for there to be an object that has F." Clearly the latter is a good deal weaker than the former and does not imply it.[3]

Necessary Knowledge versus Knowledge of Necessity

Since all of the agents that concern us here are knowers, we have it that within the framework of our system

$\Box(\forall x)(\exists t)Kxt$.

In view of the preceding relationships, this immediately yields
$(\forall x)\Box(\exists t)Kxt.$

There is no problem about a knowledge of necessity. Since we have
$p \Vdash p,$

we also have it that
$(\forall x)Kx\Box(\forall p)(p \supset p).$

And from this it follows that
$(\exists t)(\forall x)Kx\Box t.$

But is there such a thing as necessary knowledge? Can we ever have it that $\Box Kxp$? Why not? After all, there are certain facts that every knower necessarily knows, as, for example, "There are (some) facts that I know," or "Something exists," or "Some proposition is true." And this means that we will also have $(\exists t)\Box(\forall x)Kxt$ and thereby also $(\exists t)(\forall x)\Box Kxt.$

There lurks in the background here a potentially important distinction between what it is possible *for someone to know* (that is, any truth that a knower might come to cognize if afforded the requisite opportunity and means) and what it is possible *that someone knows* in the prevailing circumstances. It is possible *for* me to know what you dreamed about last night (should you choose to inform me about it—which you do not), but it is not possible *that* I have this information as things actually do and will stand. This difference between possible knowledge and learnable information is bound to figure into the larger scheme of things.

Recall that in chapter 5 we demonstrated
$\vdash (\forall t)(\forall x)Axt.$

This yields
$\vdash \Box(\forall t)(\forall x)Axt,$

which in turn yields (via the principles of QML) each of the following:
$\vdash (\forall t)\Box(\forall x)Axt$ or equivalently $\vdash \sim(\exists t)\Diamond(\exists x)Kx(\sim t)$

$\vdash (\forall t)(\forall x)\Box Axt$ or equivalently $\vdash \sim(\exists t)(\exists x)\Diamond Kx(\sim t)$

$\vdash (\forall x)\Box(\forall t)Axt$ or equivalently $\vdash \sim(\exists x)\Diamond(\exists t)Kx(\sim t)$

There is no possibility of knowing falsehoods.

Just as in epistemic contexts we cannot move inferentially from Kxp and $p \equiv q$ to Kxq, so we cannot move inferentially from $KxFu$ and $u = v$ to $KxFv$. Thus, given that 9 = the number of planets, we clearly cannot move from $Kx(9 = 9)$ to $Kx(9 = $ the number of planets). In the former case we must also require that $Kx(p \equiv q)$ and in the latter case that $Kx(u = v)$. For inferences of this kind to work, the inference-mediating facts must be known to the knowers at issue. One must recognize that modal and epistemic contexts are what is known as *nonextensional*, and that in such nonextensional contexts identity does not authorize intersubstitution. Something further is required: it is the epistemic case that the knowers at issue themselves know the facts on which we propose to draw in order to make inferences from their knowledge.

Knowledge and Modality

It might be thought that a close formal analogy obtains between semantic and epistemic necessity—between what is *necessarily* true and what is *universally known* to be so. The idea here would be to correlate $\Box p$ with $(\forall x)Kxp$, viewing this as an epistemicized mode of necessity. And on this basis we would obtain (via $\Diamond = \sim\Box\sim$) the correlation of $\Diamond p$ with $\sim(\forall x)Kxp$ or equivalently $(\exists x)Axp$ ("p is true for aught that somebody knows").

On the basis of such considerations, various theorists have over the years insisted on a close parallelism between modal and epistemic logic.[4] But this stance encounters various obstacles:

1. While the principle

"If $\vdash p$, then $\Box p$"

holds good, its epistemic analogue

"If $\vdash p$, then $(\forall x)Kxp$"

is untenable because it would impel the shift from K to K^*, impelling us in the implausible direction of logical omniscience.

2. While the principle

   "If $\Box p$ and $p \vdash q$, then $\Box q$"

holds good, its epistemic analogue

   "If $(\forall x)Kxp$ and $p \vdash q$, then $(\forall x)Kxq$"

again leads to the problematic destination of logical omniscience.

3. While the S4 principle

   $\vdash \Box p \supset \Box\Box p$

seems plausible, its epistemic analogue

   "$(\forall x)Kxp \supset (\forall x)Kx(\forall y)Kyp$,"

which transmutes universal into common knowledge, is problematic.

4. While the S5 principle

   $\vdash {\sim}\Box p \supset \Box{\sim}\Box p$

seems plausible, this is not so with its epistemic analogue:

   ${\sim}(\forall x)Kxp \supset (\forall x)Kx{\sim}(\forall y)Kyp$

or equivalently by contraposition

   $(\exists x)Ax(\forall y)Kyp \supset (\forall y)Kyp$.

This contention that when $(\forall y)Kyp$ obtains for aught that someone—some potentially ill-informed person—knows then it is actually the case is highly questionable.

All in all, then, the inclination to analogize epistemic and modal logic and to treat knowledge as a sort of modality should be resisted.

Knower Limitedness Once More

With the resources of modality at our disposal, we can now strengthen the thesis of knower limitedness—that is, $(\forall x)(\exists t){\sim}Kxt$—to

   $\Box(\forall x)(\exists t){\sim}Kxt$ or equivalently ${\sim}\Diamond(\exists x)(\forall t)Kxt$.

And, given this, QML commits us to

   $(\forall x)\Box(\exists t){\sim}Kxt$ or equivalently ${\sim}(\exists x)\Diamond(\forall t)Kxt$.

The denial of this thesis—namely, $(\exists x)\Diamond(\forall t)Kxt$, which stipulates the existence of a finite being for whom all knowledge is possibly achievable—is clearly false.

And consider also the cognate thesis:

$(\forall x)(\exists t)\Box \sim Kxt$ or equivalently $\sim(\exists x)(\forall t)\Diamond Kxt$

This denial that there is someone to whom any given truth is possibly known will also be established in chapter 13.

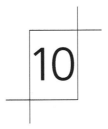

10

Problems of Epistemic Democracy

Secrets and Epistemic Democracy

A knower's secret is a truth known to this knower alone. Since (as maintained in chapter 4) the *conjunction* of everything that is known to a given knower qualifies plausibly in this regard, we should credit every knower with a secret.

And so since $(\forall x)(\exists t)(x$ alone knows $t)$ is a thesis of our system, we have it that

$\vdash \Box(\forall x)(\exists t)$ (x alone knows t).

And thus in view of the basic principles of QML we also have

$\vdash (\forall x)\Box(\exists t)$ (x alone knows t).

For every knower there necessarily is a truth known only to this individual.

Moreover, we also have it that

$\vdash (\forall x)(\exists t)\Box$ (x alone knows t).

While this thesis does not follow from the existence of secrets as such, it nevertheless does follow for cognitive exclusivity.

A *deep* secret, by contrast, is a truth that only one particular knower *can possibly* know. This, too, will be a fact of life, so that $(\exists x)(\forall t)$ $\Diamond Kxt$ is untenable.

Obviously, however, we cannot have it that "Smith knows that p_0 is a truth known to Jones alone": it is clear that a truth that involves such an exclusivity clause—on the order of "*p* is known only to Jones"—can be known by no one save the individual at issue. We must therefore accept that

$$(\forall x)(\exists t)(Kxt \,\&\, (\forall y) \sim \Diamond \,[y \neq x \,\&\, Kyt]).$$

There are thus items of knowledge—specifically those involving an exclusivity condition—that are in principle accessible only to a given individual. The idea of a cognitive democracy—that what is known can also be known by anyone else—must be abandoned.

If p_0 is a truth known to x alone and q_0 one that is known to y alone, then $p_0 \,\&\, q_0$ will be a truth that is known to no one at all. Since (as we have postulated) every knower has a secret known to himself alone, there will be a truth—namely, the conjunction of all of these—that can be known to no one at all:

$$\sim \Diamond (\forall t)(\exists x) Kxt \text{ or equivalently } \Box (\exists t)(\forall x) \sim Kxt$$

And so while it might seem plausible to contend that in principle truth is accessible to all and all alike—that no one is necessarily barred from learning any given fact—this plausible-looking contention is nevertheless untenable.

Less and More Powerful Knowers

Within the range contemplated by our epistemic logic all knowers are limited; no knower knows everything, no one is omniscient:

$$\sim (\exists x)(\forall t) Kxt \text{ or equivalently } (\forall x)(\exists t) \sim Kxt$$

And not only is no (limited) knower all knowing, but no such knower is all dominant. The existence of secrets means that no one knower knows everything known to any knower at all:

$$\sim (\exists x)(\forall t)(\forall y)(Kyt \supset Kxt) \text{ or equivalently } (\forall x)(\exists t)(\exists y)(Kyt \,\&\, \sim Kxt)$$

To be sure, some finite knowers have more powerful minds than others. But this is bound to be a matter of respect: knower x can be more powerful than y regarding matters of one type, yet knower y can be more powerful than x regarding matters of another. However, no matter how powerful a given knower is in various respects, there is always the possibility of another knower more powerful yet in all these respects. To be sure, greater power is going to be a statistical matter. For given that every knower has a secret (as shown earlier), it cannot be that a knower yet more powerful than x knows *everything* that x knows.

For aught that any finite knower knows some other finite knower may be more powerful than himself. And a less powerful knower can never fully fathom the knowledge of a more powerful one and will generally be unable to say what a more powerful intellect does or does not know. A knower whose limit is tic-tac-toe cannot comprehend the machinations of a chess master.

11

Possibility and Conceivability

Background: Possibility in Cognitive Perspective

While we learn about reality through experience, imagination is our only pathway to universal possibilities. It is thus tempting to join those theorists who hold that the merely possible stands coordinate with whatever a mind can manage to think when functioning properly—that is, to conceive coherently. They thus sought to operate with the following correlation:

Possible ≈ thinkable/conceivable

The philosopher Herbert Spencer (1820–1903), for one, effectively equated possibility with conceivability. However, other theorists, such as Edmund Husserl and Gottlob Frege, opposed such a coordination of possibility with conceivability. Conceivability, they insisted, is a psychological matter, whereas abstract possibility is something factual and objective, something independent of the concrete operations of the human mind—something that is intuited rather than imagined. There is, however, a middle way here, namely, to construe thinkability/conceivability not as a specifically human operational capacity but as something far more general, namely as matters of thinkability or conceivability *in principle* by a "mind" looked upon in a far more general and abstract way. Accordingly, explore the prospect of a theory of possibility developed with a view to an epistemological rather than psychological construal of thinkability as coherent conceivability. We thus have recourse to the idea that an object (item) is conceivable if it is in principle feasible for there to be someone—some intelligent being or other—who knows that it can (possibly) exist:

1. $Cu = \Diamond(\exists x)Kx\Diamond E!u$

On this basis, conceivability is construed in a generally *conceptual* rather than specifically *operational* sense—a matter of epistemology rather than psychology. Conceivability, in this sense, is not a matter of discussability. (After all, one can discuss such impossibilities as the "round square" of Alexius von Meinong.) Nor is it something coordinate with such psychological performances as "imagining" or "imaging." Rather, it is a fundamentally epistemic matter of what can be contemplated in a logically coherent way—of what can in principle be contemplated in thought and discourse as in items of meaningful consideration and contemplation.

In the special case of propositions, it seems appropriate to construe the actual *existence* of a proposition not in the semantical sense of a mere claim or contention but in the ontological sense of factuality or truth. On this basis we have it that a proposition "exists" when what it claims is indeed the case, that is, if it is realized *as a fact:*

2. $E!p$ iff p

Given this equivalence, (1) yields

3. $Cp = \Diamond(\exists x)Kx\Diamond p$

We thus have a uniform basis for construing conceivability either in the substantively oriented manner of (1) or in the propositionally oriented manner of (3).

Possibility in Epistemic Perspective

Such an approach to conceivability is predicated on its construal in terms of knowledge. The basic idea is that to conceive of some object is to know it to be possible, so that for an individual x to conceive of an item u is to realize that its existence is possible. On this basis, we can now readily move from the preceding specification of conceivability in general to the specific case of propositional conceivability. For we now have

4. Cp iff $\Diamond(\exists x)Kx\Diamond p$

A proposition in sum is conceivable if it is possible for its possibility to be known.

Let now return to the starting point of the present deliberations with its basic correlation of possibility with conceivability:

Possible $\approx$ thinkable/conceivable

Given this coordination, we can now contemplate the following correlation:

(C) $\Diamond p$ iff Cp

That is, we can—as per the first section, above—coordinate possibility with conceivability in the epistemic sense of this term. And in light of (4) above, (C) leads to

5. $\Diamond p$ iff $\Diamond(\exists x)Kx\Diamond p$

This, of course, is not a *definition* of possibility—as such it would clearly be circular—but rather constitutes a general principle that governs its modus operandi as yet another principle of epistemic logic.

Ramifications

It may be asked whether (5) is to be seen as a particular consequence of

6. p iff $\Diamond(\exists x)Kxp$

via the substitution $\Diamond p/p$. The answer is an emphatic no, because it is clear that (6) does not hold. For if it did, this would entail

7. $(\forall t)\Diamond(\exists x)Kxt.$

And as we have seen, this thesis is certainly not tenable for finite knowers. (See chapter 12.) But, of course, (5), which is emphatically weaker than (6), is something else altogether. It is clear that (5) splits into two components, the first of which is

5.1. $\Diamond p \supset \Diamond(\exists x)Kx\Diamond p$ or equivalently $\Box(\forall x)\sim Kx\sim p \supset \Box p$ or equivalently $\Box(\forall x)Axp \supset \Box p$.

This comes down to the thesis that the only necessary propositions are those that are *of necessity* true for aught that anyone knows.

To be sure, it is the case that

$(\forall x)Axp \supset p$

is false. But thesis (5.1) is a significant weakening of this and qualifies as an independently tenable principle of epistemic logic. We cannot maintain that all truth is possibly known to be true, but there is no problem with the contention that all possibility is possibly known to be possible.

Let us turn to the converse of (5.1), namely,

5.2. $\Diamond(\exists x)Kx\Diamond p \supset \Diamond p$ or equivalently $\Box p \supset \Box(\forall x)\ Ax\Box p$.

Since we have it as a theorem that

8. $p \supset (\forall x)Axp$

obtains, this thesis (5.2) follows by QML.

So once (5.1) is accepted, it is altogether plausible to accept the whole of (5) as an appropriate thesis of epistemic modal logic. And in line with this we can indeed endorse the epistemic construal of possibility contemplated in the first section, above, and—in adopting principle (C)—proceed to endorse conceivability-in-principle as a viable epistemic version of possibility.

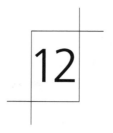

Unknowability

The Knowability Thesis

Clearly, we cannot, on grounds of self-inconsistency, have it that someone *knows* some truth to represent an unknown fact:

$(\exists x)(\exists p)Kx(p \ \& \sim (\exists y)Kyp)$ or equivalently $(\exists x)(\exists p)(Kxp \ \& \ Kx\sim(\exists y)Kyp)$

This thesis must certainly be rejected. But its weaker cousin, to the effect that there indeed is such a thing as an unknown fact—that is,

$(\exists x)(\exists p)(p \ \& \ Kx\sim(\exists y)Kyp)$ or equivalently $(\exists x)(\exists t)Kx$ $\sim(\exists y)Kyt$

is perfectly tenable. We have to come to terms with the existence of unknowns.

With finite knowers we can never have a thesis of the format $(\forall p)KxF(p)$ or $(\forall t)KxF(t)$, owing to the infinitude of that quantificational range. Accordingly, we have it that

$\sim\Diamond(\exists x)(\forall t)KxF(t),$

so that in consequence

$\Box(\forall x)(\exists t)\sim KxF(t)$

obtains irrespective of F. Thus, with $F(t) = t$ in particular we have
$$\Box(\forall x)(\exists t)\sim Kxt$$

and consequently also
$$(\forall x)\Box(\exists t)\sim Kxt.$$

We have already noted (in chapter 8) the need to reject the contention that all truth is known, so that the thesis $(\forall t)(\exists x)Kxt$ is unacceptable. After all, there is good reason to think that the range of human knowledge is limited and that there are true facts that we shall never know. But of late there has been increasing interest in the prospect of establishing the reality of unknown and indeed unknowable truth on the basis of very abstract and general considerations of epistemic logic, with several theorists contending that it can readily be demonstrated in this way that unknowable truth is an inescapable feature of our cognitive condition.[1]

The root source of this conviction lies in the circumstance that in 1963 the Yale logician Frederic B. Fitch published a brief paper demonstrating on very general principles that there must be unknown truths.[2] Since Fitch's analysis did not stress the point and seemed preoccupied with other issues, this startling result lay dormant until W. D. Hart drew attention to it in 1979.[3] In the 1980s deliberations regarding various ramifications of Fitch's insights were projected by J. J. MacIntosh, Richard Routley, Timothy Williamson, myself, and others. Let us consider where the issue of demonstrating the existence of unknowable truth is left in light of this discussion and inquire into the status of the *knowability thesis*, to the effect that *any true proposition can possibly be known.* Can this idea be substantiated?

Observe, to begin with, that this thesis is equivocal and can bear different constructions according as one attaches an explanatory rider, such as "by any individual" or "by some individual or other." In fact, four alternatives arise:

I. $(\forall t)(\forall x)\Diamond Kxt$ or equivalently $\sim(\exists t)(\exists x)\Box\sim Kxt$
II. $(\forall t)\Diamond(\forall x)Kxt$ or equivalently $\sim(\exists t)\Box(\exists x)\sim Kxt$
III. $(\forall t)(\exists x)\Diamond Kxt$ or equivalently $\sim(\exists t)(\forall x)\Box\sim Kxt$
IV. $(\forall t)\Diamond(\exists x)Kxt$ or equivalently $\sim(\exists t)\Box(\forall x)\sim Kxt$

The four theses of this spectrum are not, of course, logically independent. It lies in the quantified modal logic of things that the following deductive relationships must obtain:

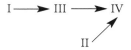

So the question now emerges: In which of these versions (if any) is the *knowability thesis* acceptable?[4]

Modal Collapse

The subsequent discussion will make use of the following *Modal Collapse theorem* (due to J. J. MacIntosh, 1984).[5] Let F be any propositional qualifier ("modality") obeying the following three principles:

(C) $F(p \& q) \supset (Fp \& Fq)$ *conjunction principle*
(V) $Fp \supset p$ *veracity principle*
(P) $p \supset \Diamond Fp$ *possibility principle*[6]

Then F characterizes all truths. That is, it will be provable that $p \supset Fp$ or equivalently $(\forall t)Ft$.

Proof:

1. $F(p \& \sim Fp) \supset$ $(Fp \& F\sim Fp)$	from (C) via the substitution $\sim Fp/q$
2. $F\sim Fp \supset \sim Fp$	from (V) via the substitution $\sim Fp/p$
3. $\sim F(p \& \sim Fp)$	since (2) amounts to the negation of (1)'s consequent
4. $\square \sim F(p \& \sim Fp)$	from (3) by necessitation
5. $\sim \Diamond F(p \& \sim Fp)$	from (4) by modal logic
6. $(p \& \sim Fp) \supset \Diamond F$ $(p \& \sim Fp)$	from (P) via the substitution $(p \& \sim Fp)/p$
7. $\sim (p \& \sim Fp)$	from (5), (6)
8. $p \supset Fp$	from (7) QED

Given both (C) and (V), we have, in effect derived $(\forall t)Ft$ from $(\forall t)\Diamond Ft$.

The Knowability Thesis in Trouble

Let us put the Modal Collapse theorem to work via the specification

$Fp = (\exists x)Kxp.$

Observe that now (P) amounts to

$(\forall t)\Diamond(\exists x)Kxt$ or equivalently $\sim(\exists t)\Box(\forall x)\sim Kxt,$

which is to say that (P) comes to thesis IV. Seeing that (C) and (V) both obviously obtain with this present construal of F, the Modal Collapse theorem yields

$(\forall t)(\exists x)Kxt.$

Since this IV-consequence to the effect that all truths are known is clearly unacceptable, so is IV itself.

This finding at one stroke invalidates the entire quartet at issue in the thesis spectrum discussed in the first section. The *knowability thesis* is unacceptable in all its forms. In particular, it follows from not-IV that with finite knowers there will be truths that no one can possibly know to be such. And this finding should not be all that surprising, for since each knower has a secret, as has been insisted throughout (see chapter 4), the conjunction of all of these secrets will, as already noted, be a truth known to no one at all.

13

Fitch's Theorem and Its Consequences

The Import of Fitch's Theorem

The findings on unknowability discussed in the preceding chapter have interesting ramifications. Thus, consider yet another application of the Modal Collapse theorem, namely, that arising with the following specification of *F*:

$Fp = Kxp$

The theorem's grounding principles (of conjunction and veracity) now both obtain once again, so that

If $(\forall t)\Diamond Kxt$, then $(\forall t)Kxt$.

Now one certainly does not have it in general that

If $(\forall u)\Diamond Fu$, then $(\forall u)Fu$.

In this light the aforementioned implication thesis is extraordinary and may seem surprising.

The implication thesis at issue—initially established by Fitch in 1963—might be called Fitch's theorem. For all intents and purposes it says that if every truth is *possibly* known to someone, then every truth is *actually* known to this individual. So insofar as one is minded to

deny the latter, as one must, the former has to be rejected as well. Accordingly, $(\exists x)(\forall t)\Diamond Kxt$ must be rejected so that we have
$(\forall x)(\exists t)\Box \sim Kxt.$

In the domain of our system, every knower is necessarily imperfect in the manner of this thesis, that is, in there being some truth that is necessarily not known to him. And so the prospect of knowledge unrestrictedly open to all is no go. And note further that Fitch's theorem has the consequence
$(\forall t)\Diamond Kxt \vdash \Diamond(\forall t)Kxt,$

whose generic analogue
$(\forall u)\Diamond Fu \vdash \Diamond(\forall u)Fu$

certainly does not obtain (see chapter 10).
   Fitch's theorem does *not*, of course, mean that we have the clearly untenable
$(\forall t)(\Diamond Kxt \supset Kxt).$

Nor does it mean that we have
$(\exists x)\Diamond Kxt \supset (\exists x)Kxt.$[1]

But what it does accomplish by way of a transit from possibility to actuality nevertheless has an anomalous air about it. Be this as it may, since we have little alternative but to reject $(\exists x)(\forall t)Kxt$, Fitch's theorem means that we have no choice about also rejecting
$(\exists x)(\forall t)\Diamond Kxt.$

And so we must accept its negation:
$(\forall x)(\exists t)\sim\Diamond Kxt$ or equivalently $(\forall x)(\exists t)\Box \sim Kxt$

For every finite knower there is something unknowable—some person-specific unknowable fact that this individual cannot know. All limited knowers have cognitive blind spots: For every finite knower there is some person-correlative unknowable—a truth that this individual cannot possibly know.[2]

Moreover, Fitch's theorem should not really be seen as all that surprising. For suppose x is a limited knower. Then $(\exists t) \sim Kxt$. So let t_0 be such a truth that x does not know: $\sim Kxt_0$. And now consider the truth: $t_0 \& \sim Kxt_0$. Clearly, x cannot possibly know *this* truth, since $Kx(t_0 \& \sim Kxt_0)$ is self-contradictory. So we have it that $(\exists t) \sim \Diamond Kxt$. But observe that we have now effectively established

$(\exists t) \sim Kxt \vdash (\exists t) \sim \Diamond Kxt$ or equivalently (by contraposition) $(\forall t) \Diamond Kxt \vdash (\forall t) Kxt$. QED.

Fitch's theorem in effect establishes a collective incompatibility among the following four theses:

- (F)   Knower finitude
  $(\forall x)(\exists t) \sim Kxt$
- (C)   The conjunction principle
  $Kx(p \& q) \supset (Kxp \& Kxq)$
- (V)   The veracity principle
  $Kxp \supset p$
- (K)   The *knowability principle*
  $p \supset \Diamond Kxp$ or equivalently $(\forall t) \Diamond Kxt$

Accordingly, one or another of these plausible-seeming theses must be rejected. This situation is sometimes characterized as "Fitch's paradox."[3] However, our present treatment of epistemic logic does not see this situation as paradoxical but rather as a token of the ultimately not implausible circumstance that for the reasons of the already indicted sort (K), the *knowability principle* must be abandoned.

Seeking an Unknowable Truth

Of course, x cannot know y's secrets. But are there also truths that no one whatsoever can possibly know? Can we maintain the thesis that $(\exists t)(\forall x) \sim \Diamond Kxt$ or equivalently $(\exists t)(\forall x) \Box \sim Kxt$ or $\sim (\forall t)(\exists x) \Diamond Kxt$?

The thesis $(\forall x)(\exists t) \Box \sim Kxt$ established above means that for any limited knower x_i there will be some truth—let it be t_i—that of necessity x_i does not know, so that $\Box \sim Kx_i t_i$ will obtain. Let t^* be the grand *conjunction* of all of these truths t_i for our (finitely many) knowers x_i. Then clearly *this* truth will be one that, of necessity, none of our knowers can possibly know. Thus, clearly, this grand conjunctive truth consisting of the personalized necessarily unknown truths of all of our limited knowers will be necessarily unknown across-the-board: $(\forall x)\Box \sim Kxt^*$. With limited knowers, then, there are not only unknown but even unknowable truths:

$(\exists t)(\forall x)\Box \sim Kxt$ so that $\sim (\forall t)(\exists x)\Diamond Kxt$

However, the question now arises: what would be a plausible candidate for such an unknowable truth? Can a specific example be provided? The answer is no. An unknowable truth cannot possibly be identified as such. For in the very act of establishing that a certain statement qualifies as a truth, we would unravel its unknowability. In adducing, say t_0, as a certifiable example of such an unknowable truth we ourselves (*i*) claim to know t_0 & $\sim(\exists x)Kxt_0$. That is, with respect to ourselves, *i*, we have

$Ki(t_0$ & $\sim(\exists x)Kxt_0)$.

And this contention is self-contradictory. (Note, however, that in claiming this condition for the t^* indicated above we have merely indicated t^* by a description that, while indeed unique to it, nevertheless does not specifically identify it.[4])

The fact of the matter is that the preceding argument establishes that

$Ki(\exists p)(p$ & $(\forall x) \sim \Diamond Kxp)$,
where $i =$ oneself.

But we cannot possibly particularize that unknown item, exchanging Ki and $(\exists p)$ so as to move to

$(\exists p)Ki(p$ & $(\forall x) \sim \Diamond Kxp)$.

For this proposition straightaway entails the existence of a proposition p for which we have both Kip and $(\forall x) \sim \Diamond Kxp$, which is clearly impossible. And the same result holds when one shifts from oneself to some other individual. (The order of K and $\exists$ is the crucial factor here.)

And so while unknowability is something we can establish in the abstract, illustrating its realization in the concrete is something we cannot achieve. When finite knowers confront an infinite manifold of distinct truths, it transpires that while there must be (infinitely many) truths that they cannot specifically know to be such, there will nevertheless not be a single certifiable instance of this. Here we once more have it that *that* knowledge is one thing and *what* knowledge something else again. Nobody does—or even can—know of a particular proposition that it is actually an unknowable truth. Thus, even when $\Box(\exists t)\sim Kit$ is assured, one remains unable to *identify* the unknown at issue, and so cannot maintain $(\exists t)\Box\sim Kit$ (let alone find a particular t_0 for which $\Box\sim Kit_0$).

Yet what of the situation of *other* people's ignorance? Of course, x can know that y does not know some truth. There is no difficulty with $Kx\sim Kyt$. But what of x's knowing that y is *necessarily* ignorant of some truth—what of $Kx\Box\sim Kyt$? Can we have

$(\exists t)(\exists x)(\exists y)Kx\Box\sim Kyt$ or equivalently $(\exists t)(\exists x)(\exists y)Kx\sim\Diamond Kyt$?

Indeed, we can; there is no difficulty here. This can be demonstrated as follows. Let t_0 be a truth unknown to y. Then

1. $t_1 = (t_0 \& \sim Kyt_0)$ is a true proposition that y cannot possibly know.
2. $Ki\sim\Diamond Kyt_1$ from (1)
3. $(\exists t)Ki\sim\Diamond Kyt$ from (2)
4. $(\exists t)(\exists x)Kx\sim\Diamond Kyt$ from (3)
5. $(\exists t)(\exists x)(\exists y)Kx\sim\Diamond Kyt$ from (4) QED

Knowledge of necessary ignorance is unquestionably feasible. Moreover, since the i of this course of reasoning is generic, it is clear that the argument just given would also serve to establish $(\exists t)(\forall x)(\exists y)Kx\sim\Diamond Kyt$.

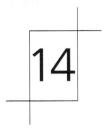

Finite and Infinite Knowers

Finite and Infinite Knowers: Distributive versus Collective Knowledge

The difference between a finite and an infinite knower is of far-reaching importance and requires careful elucidation. For an "infinite knower" should not be construed as an *omniscient* knower—one from whom nothing knowable is concealed (and so who knows, for example, who will be elected U.S. president in the year 2200). Rather, what is now at issue is a knower who can manage to know in individualized detail an infinite number of independent facts. Such a knower might, for example, be able to answer such a question as "Will the decimal expansion of π always continue to agree for one hundred decimal places at some future point with that of $\sqrt{2}$?" (And, of course, the circumstance that an infinite knower can know *some* infinite set of independent facts does not mean that the knower can know *every* such set.)

Can a finite knower know a universal truth—one of potentially infinite range? This is clearly a critically important issue, seeing that laws of nature are propositions of just this sort. Fortunately, the answer here is an affirmative. After all, once we acknowledge the prospect of an inductively based knowledge of general laws, we will have it that a knower can unproblematically know—for example, that "All dogs are mammals." A true proposition of the format $(\forall u)\,Fu$—which encompasses $(\forall v)(Gv \supset Hv)$—is a format that is in principle available to such knowers. And so general knowledge, knowledge of universal facts, in the manner of $Kx(\forall u)Fu$, will, on any ordinary view of the matter, be accessible to finite intelligences.[1]

But what a finite knower *cannot* do is to know this sort of thing *in detail* rather than at the level of generality. For, as already noted in chapter 8, distributive knowledge of universal facts over an infinite or indefinite range is beyond the reach of a finite knower. No such knower can know specifically of each and every u in that potentially infinite range that Fu obtains—that is, while he can know collectively *that all* individuals u have F, he cannot know distributively *of* every u that *it* has F. One can certainly know (through the U.S. Constitution) *that* every president is native born. But, of course, one has this knowledge without knowing *of* every president (including those one has never heard of, let alone those yet unborn) that each individual one of them is native born—something one cannot do without knowing who they are.

This distinction between collective and distributive knowledge means that, while there is no problem with (for example) the thesis
$$(\exists x)Kx(\forall p)(p \supset p),$$

nevertheless, the situation is different with the *cognate thesis*
$$(\exists x)(\forall p)Kx(p \supset p).$$

This will not be acceptable, because the infinitude of that propositional range outruns x's cognitive reach. And in rejecting this, we will have no choice but to endorse
$$(\forall x){\sim}(\forall p)Kx(p \supset p) \text{ or equivalently } (\forall x)(\exists p){\sim}Kx(p \supset p).$$

With finite knowers there are going to be patently true propositions that they do not know specifically and distributively but rather only in the collective mode, through their knowledge of general principles. No doubt all propositions of this format $(p \supset p)$ are potentially knowable for a finite knower: he can in theory know *any one* of them. But what he cannot do is manage to know specifically *the entire lot* of them.

Pi Knowledge

It is worthwhile to explore the implications of dealing specifically with a finite set of finite knowers (such as we must presume *Homo sapiens* represent). Let $\pi(j)$ be the digit occupying the j-th place in the decimal expansion of π. Then supposing, as we have, that there is a finite number of finite knowers, there will be a largest value of j such that $\pi(j)$ is ever specifically identified by any knower. Let this largest value be n. Accordingly, we shall have

$$(\forall u) \sim (\exists x) Kx(\pi(n+1) = u).$$

To be sure, with an infinite number of finite knowers no such n need be defined. Nor need it be defined with a finite (or infinite) number of infinite knowers. But these involve conditions contrary to fact and with finitely many finite knowers, n stands firmly in place.

And so we have it that in a finite community of finite knowers no one will ever know the value of $\pi(n+1)$:

$$\sim (\exists x) Kx \text{ (the digital value of } \pi(n+1))$$

This is a truth: nobody knows that fact. But what of the contention that no one *can* ever know it? Is it the case that

$$\sim \Diamond (\exists x) Kx \text{ (the digital value of } \pi(n+1))?$$

This, of course, by no means follows. That no one *does* do something does not rule out the possibility that someone *might*.

With the assertion $(\exists x) Kxp$ or even $(\exists x) \Diamond Kxp$ we contemplate a finite population of knowers. And there is a limit to what such knowers can know. But when we shift to $\Diamond (\exists x) Kxp$, this limitation is abrogated. Even if all the knowers we are prepared to contemplate are finite knowers, there is no limit of finitude to the range of facts such knowers might *possibly* realize.

But let us consider a cognate issue, now adopting the abbreviation $\Pi(j)$ = the true statement that the value of $\pi(j)$ is whatever it in fact happens to be.

Then as we have seen
$$\sim(\exists x)Kx\Pi(n+1),$$

and so once again $(\exists t) \sim (\exists x)Kxt$ or equivalently $(\exists t)(\forall x)\sim Kxt$. Now here
$$\lozenge(\exists x)Kx\,\Pi(n+1)$$

is certainly the case: it is uncontestably possible that a finite knower could know $\Pi(n+1)$. For in principle (finite) knowers might conceivably push things a bit further. There is no specifiable j such that $\Pi(j)$ necessarily lies outside the cognitive reach of every (finite) knower. However, what cannot possibly be the case with finite knowers is
$$(\exists x)(\forall j)Kx\Pi(j).$$

(Though with *infinite* knowers this may well be true.)
But now what of
$$(\forall j)\lozenge(\exists x)Kx\Pi(j)?$$

This will clearly be true even when we are dealing with a finite set of finite knowers, where we are bound to have
$$\sim\lozenge(\forall j)(\exists x)Kx\Pi(j).$$

Nevertheless, with an infinite family of finite knowers it may well be true so that here we will indeed have
$$\lozenge(\forall j)(\exists x)Kx\Pi(j).$$

Thus, while there is no limit to facts of the $\Pi(j)$ range that lie within the reach of finite knowers, it nevertheless remains that
$$\lozenge(\exists x)(\forall j)Kx\Pi(j)$$

is not a tenable thesis. And even with infinitely many finite knowers we shall not have this thesis: to obtain it would require the shift to infinite knowers.
The fact that $\lozenge(\exists x)(\forall i)Kx\Pi(j)$ is not tenable means that neither is
$$\lozenge(\exists x)(\forall t)Kxt.$$

And so we have

$\sim\Diamond(\exists x)(\forall t)Kx$ or equivalently $\Box(\forall x)(\exists t)\sim Kxt$.

This thesis is in effect a stronger version of knower limitedness, seeing that it goes beyond $(\forall x)(\exists t)\sim Kxt$ to entail $(\forall x)\Box(\exists t)\sim Kxt$.

Another Perspective on the Limitations of Finite Knowers

Let $t_1, t_2, t_3, \ldots$ be an infinite series of nonredundant truths so that no t_i follows inferentially from the conjunction of what precedes. Then, supposing once more that we have a deal with a finite set of finite knowers, there will have to be some integer N such that for no $i \geq N$ is t_i known to any knower. Now let n be the smallest such N. Then

$\sim(\exists x)Kxt_n$

But now what about the thesis

$\Diamond(\exists x)Kxt_n$?

At this point the situation becomes much like that for π knowledge as discussed above, and the previous deliberations can be carried over with appropriate adjustments. We arrive at

$\sim(\forall t)\Diamond(\exists x)Kxt$.

After all, even when a knower can know *any* truth of the series t_1, t_2, t_3, . .—no matter how far out—as long as he cannot specifically know *every* truth in the series there will be certain determinations about the series as a whole that he is unable to make.

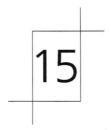

15

Vagrant Predicates
and Noninstantiability

Noninstantiable Properties

One can refer to an item in two distinctly different ways: either
specifically and individually by means of naming or identifying characterizations ("George Washington, the father of our country"), or
obliquely and sortally as an item of a certain type or kind ("an American male born in the eighteenth century"). Now, a peculiar and interesting mode of reference occurs when an item is referred to obliquely in such a way that its specific identification is flat-out precluded as
a matter of principle. This phenomenon is illustrated by claims to the
existence of

- a thing whose identity will never be known
- an idea that has never occurred to anybody
- an occurrence that no one has ever mentioned
- an integer that is never individually specified

Here, those particular items that render $(\exists u)Fu$ true are *referentially
inaccessible:* to indicate them individually and specifically as instances
of the predicate at issue is ipso facto to unravel them as so-character-
ized items.[1]

The concept of an applicable but nevertheless noninstantiable predicate comes to view at this point. This is a predicate F whose realization is noninstantiable because, while it is true *in abstracto* that this property is exemplified—that is, $(\exists u)Fu$ will be true—nevertheless, the very manner of its specification makes it impossible to identify any particular individual u_0 such that Fu_0 obtains. Accordingly,

F is a *vagrant* predicate iff $(\exists u)Fu$ is true, while, nevertheless, Fu_0 is false for each and every specifically identified u_0.

Such predicates are "vagrant" in the sense of *having no known address or fixed abode:* though they indeed have applications, these cannot be specifically instanced—they cannot be pinned down and located in a particular spot. Predicates of this sort will be such that one can show on the basis of general principles that there must be items to which they apply, while, nevertheless, one can also establish that no such items can ever be concretely identified.[2]

Examples of Vagrant Predicates

The following predicates present properties that are clearly noninstantiable in this way:

- being an ever-unstated (proposition, theory).
- being a never-mentioned topic (idea, object).
- being a truth (a fact) no one has ever realized (learned, stated).
- being someone whom everyone has forgotten.
- being a never-identified culprit.
- being an issue no one has thought about since the sixteenth century.

Noninstantiability itself is certainly not something that is noninstantiable: many instances can be given. Specifically, in our epistemic context, one realizes perfectly well that there are bound to be truths one does not know,

$(\exists p)(p \ \& \sim\! Kip).$

But, of course, I can identify no such specific p_0 for which I know

$p_0 \ \& \sim\! Kip_0.$

Thus, while
$$(\exists x)Kx(\exists p)(p \mathbin{\&} \sim Kxp)$$

can be maintained unproblematically,
$$(\exists x)(\exists p)Kx(p \mathbin{\&} \sim Kxp)$$

cannot because it straightaway engenders a contradiction. The generic p at issue in that former thesis is thus in principle noninstantiable.

There are bound to be truths nobody knows. But no one can provide a certifiable instance of this phenomenon, so that

being a truth nobody knows

is a model instance of a vagrant predicate.

The Role of General Principles in Validating Claims of Inapplicability

A predicate F is *generically applicable* when we have
$$(\exists u)Fu.$$

On the other hand, a predicate is *specifically instantiated* if we manage to indicate its concretely identified application in some particular instance,

for some canonically identified u_0, Fu_0.

After all, it is useful—indeed, necessary—to distinguish between a property F that is known to have an application
$$(\exists x)Kx(\exists u)Fu$$

and there being a *known* instance of F:
$$(\exists u)(Fu \mathbin{\&} (\exists x)KxFu) \text{ or simply } (\exists u)(\exists x)KxFu.$$

In the former case we only know that there is a fact; in the latter there is a *known* fact. And, of course, there are doubtless facts of this nature that are not and indeed cannot be identifiably known. When something of the kind typified by "unknown instance" occurs, we have to do with vagrant predicates: they exist in the gap established by the distinction at issue.

The existence of vagrant predicates shows that applicability and instantiability do not come to the same thing. By definition, vagrant predicates will be applicable: there, indeed, are items to which they apply. However, this circumstance will always have to be something that must be claimed on the basis of general principles, basing it on concretely identified instances is, by hypothesis, infeasible.

Consider an example of this sort of general-principle demonstration. There are infinitely many positive integers. But the earth has a beginning and end in time. Its overall history has room for only a finite number of intelligent earthlings, each of whom can only make specific mention of a finite number of integers. (They can, of course, refer to the set of integers at large, but they can only specifically take note of a finite number of them.) There will accordingly be some ever unmentioned, ever unconsidered integers—indeed, an infinite number of them. But clearly no one can give a specific example of this.

Or again consider

being an unverified truth.

Since in the history of the species there can only be a finite number of specifically verified propositions, while actual truths must be infinite in number, we know that there will be some such unverified truths. But to say specifically of a particular proposition that it is an unverified truth is impracticable, seeing that doing so involves claiming it as a truth and thereby classing it as a proposition whose truth has been determined. We can allude to such items but cannot actually identify them. Such examples show how considerations of general principle can substantiate claims to the existence of vagrant predicates.

General versus Specific Knowledge and the Impact of Vagrancy

The difference between predicate vagrancy and its contrary mirrors the difference encountered in chapter 8 between

Generic knowledge: I know that something *F*'s: $Ki(\exists u)Fu$

and

> *Specific knowledge:* I know something that *F*'s; that is, I know of
> something that it(!) *F*'s: $(\exists u) KiFu$

This recurs at the general level in the distinction between the generic
"Somebody knows that something has *F*,"

$(\exists x) Kx (\exists u) Fu,$

in contrast to the specific "There is something of which someone
knows that it in particular has *F*,"

$(\exists x)(\exists u) KxFu.$

In the former case *y* simply knows that *F* is applicable; in the latter case
x is in a position to adduce specific example *F*-application—to adduce
a *known instance* of *F*. From the logical standpoint, then, the issue
comes down to the relative placement of the existential quantifier and
the cognitive operator. It is in just this context that vagrancy manifests
itself.

Vagrant predicates are by nature noninstantiable, but we can nevertheless use them to *individuate* items that we can never *identify*. (Recall the discussion of this distinction in chapter 7.) Thus, if someone
is specified as "the oldest unknown (that is, never-to-be-identified)
victim of the "eruption of Krakatoa," then we can make various true
claims about the so-individuated person—for example, that this individual was alive at the time of Krakatoa's eruption. We can allude to
that person but by hypothesis cannot manage to identify him. Predicative vagrancy thus reinforces the distinction between mere individ-
uation and actual identification.

Vagrant Predicates as Epistemic

To establish vagrancy for a predicate *F* one needs to show that
while there indeed are *F*-instantiating items, nevertheless, they cannot
be specifically identified, so that their status as such is never known.
This comes to maintaining

$(\exists u)(Fu \ \& \sim (\exists x) KxFu).$

No problem here. Such a claim makes perfectly good sense.

It would not, however, make sense for us (or anyone) to claim to know the identity of this unknown. That is, we could not sensibly claim that for some specified individual u_0

$$Fu_0 \ \& \ \sim(\exists x)KxFu_0.$$

For maintaining this—and thereby maintaining Fu_0—commits us to the claim that we ourselves know Fu_0 to be the case so that $KiFu_0$ ($i =$ myself). But then in going on to say $\sim(\exists x)KxFu_0$ we stand committed to denying this claim and thereby enmesh ourselves in contradiction. In other words, $Ki(Fu \ \& \sim(\exists x)KxFu_0)$ is incoherent.

The fact is that whenever F is a vagrant predicate the claim that

$$(\exists x)(\exists u)KxFu$$

is (by hypothesis) in principle self-contradictory and thereby false. Accordingly, there is something about F that renders it by nature inaccessible to knowledge and that, in consequence, endows it with inherently epistemic involvements.

With formalistic discussions in matters of logic or mathematics—where predicates cast in the language of cognitive operators have no place—one never encounters vagrant predicates. For in such contexts we affirm *what* we know but never claim *that* we know. However, with epistemic matters the situation can be very different.

Consider such predicates as
- being a book no one has ever read.
- being a sunset never witnessed by any member of *Homo sapiens*.

Such items may be difficult to instantiate—but certainly not impossible. The former could be instantiated by author and title; the latter by place and date. In neither case would its instantiation unravel that item as described. Being read is not indispensably essential to books, nor is being seen to sunsets: being an unread book or an unwitnessed sunset involves no contradiction in terms. But in those epistemic cases that concern us now, epistemic inaccessibility is built into the specification at issue. Here, being instantiated stands in direct logical conflict with the characterization at issue, as with

- being a person who has passed into total oblivion
- being a never-formulated question
- being an idea no one any longer mentions

To identify such an item (in the way now at issue) is thereby to unravel its specifying characterization.[3]

The knowledge operator K is of the essence here. What is pivotal in all of these cases of vagrant predicates is that they involve a specification that—like identification, comprehension, formulation, and mention—is fundamentally epistemic, something that can only be performed by a creature capable of cognitive and communicative performances. This is readily established. Let F be a vagrant predicate. Since we then by hypothesis have it that $(\exists u)Fu$ is true, there is clearly nothing impossible about being F-possession as such. Ontologically speaking, there are, by hypothesis, items to which F applies; what is infeasible is only providing an instance—a specific example or illustration. The impossibility lies not in "being an F" as such but in "being an concretely/instantiated F." The problem is not with the indefinite "*something* is an F" but with the specific "*this* is an F." Difficulty lies not with F-hood as such but with its specific application—not with the ontology of there being an F but with the epistemology of its apprehension in individual cases.

The Centrality of Epistemic Involvement

The salient point is that specification, exemplification, and so on are epistemic processes that, as such, are incompatible with those epistemically voided characterizations provided by vagrant predicates. Total oblivion and utter nonentertainment are automatically at odds with identificatory instantiation. After all, honoring a request to identify the possessor of an noninstantiable property is simply impossible. For any such response would be self-defeating.

It is this uniting, common feature of all vagrant predicates that they are so specified that in the very act of identifying a would-be instantiation of them we will automatically violate—that is, falsify—one of the definitive features of the specification at issue. In other words, with such noninstantiable features their noninstantiability is something inherent in the defining specification of the features at issue.

Specifically, in claiming F to be instanced but not instantiable we subscribe to

$(\exists u)(Fu \,\&\, {\sim}\Diamond(\exists x)KxFu).$

Accordingly, let us define this idea of "being an unknown instance of $F^{\#}$" by the specification

$F^{\#}u$ iff $Fu \,\&\, {\sim}\Diamond(\exists x)KxFu.$

On this basis, the aforementioned contention that F has an unknown instance comes to $(\exists u)F^{\#}u$. And to say that this itself is known is perfectly practicable. For

$(\exists x)Kx(\exists u)F^{\#}u$ or equivalently $(\exists x)Kx(\exists u)(Fu \,\&\, {\sim}\Diamond(\exists y)KyFu)$

is a perfectly viable contention.[4]

The very concept of instantiability/noninstantiability is thus epistemic in its bearing because all of the relevant procedures—exemplifying, illustrating, identifying, naming, mentioning, and the like—are inherently referential by way of purporting a knowledge of identity. And since all such referential processes are mind projected—and cannot but be so—they are epistemic in nature. On this basis, the idea of knowledge is unavoidably present throughout the phenomenon of predicative vagrancy.

Concrete versus Generic Knowledge and Ignorance

Vagrant predicates betoken the unavoidability of areas of ignorance. And, indeed, one of the most critical but yet problematic areas of inquiry relates to knowledge regarding our own cognitive shortcomings. To be sure, there is no problem with the idea that Q is a question we cannot answer. But it is next to impossible to get a more definite fix on our own ignorance, because in order even to know that there is a certain particular fact that we do not know, we would have to know the item at issue to be a fact, and just this is, by hypothesis, something we do not know.[5]

And these considerations bear directly on our present deliberations. There, indeed, are truths that nobody can know, so that we have $Ki(\exists p)(p \,\&\, \sim\!\Diamond(\exists x)Kxp)$. But, of course, we do not have the possibility of illustrating this, seeing that the thesis

$$(\exists p)Ki(p \,\&\, \sim\!\Diamond(\exists x)Kxp)$$

is untenable on grounds of self-inconsistency. Here, we cannot interchange that Ki with its subsequent $(\exists p)$.

And so "being a fact I do not know" is a noninstantiable predicate as far as I am concerned. (You, of course, could proceed to instantiate it.) But "being a fact that *nobody* knows is flat-out noninstantiable—so here we have a typical vagrant predicate.

Correspondingly, one must recognize that there is a crucial difference between the indefinite "I know that there is some fact that I do not (or cannot) know" and the specific "Such and such is a fact of which I know that I do not know it." The first is unproblematic but the second is not, seeing that to know of something that it is a fact I must know it as such so that what is at issue is effectively a contradiction in terms.

Accordingly, it lies in the nature of things that my ignorance about facts is something regarding what one can have only generic and not specific knowledge. I can know about my ignorance only abstractly at the level of indefiniteness (*sub ratione generalitatis*), but I cannot know it in concrete detail. I can meaningfully hold that two and two's being four is a *claim* (or a *purported* fact) that I do not know to be the case but cannot meaningfully maintain that two and two's being four is an *actual* fact that I do not know to be the case. To maintain a fact as fact is to assert knowledge of it: in maintaining p as a fact one claims to know that p. One can know *that* one does not know various truths but is not in a position to *identify* any of the specific truths one does not know. In sum, I can have general but not specific knowledge about my ignorance, although my knowledge about *your* ignorance is unproblematic in this regard.[6]

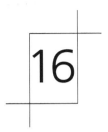

Unanswerable Questions and Insolubilia

Questions and Answers

It is instructive to adopt an erotetic—that is, question-oriented—view of knowledge and ignorance. It can be supposed, without loss of generality, that the answers to questions are always complete propositions. Often, to be sure, it appears on the surface that a specific item is merely at issue with a question, as in the following example:

Q: "Who is that man?"
A: "Tom Jones."
Q: "When will he come?"
A: "At two o'clock."
Q: "What prime numbers lie between two and eight?"
A: "Three, five, and seven."

But, throughout, the answers can be recast as completed propositions, respectively: "That man is Tom Jones"; "He will come at two o'clock"; "Three, five, and seven are the prime numbers between two and eight." So we shall here take the line that the answers to questions are given as complete propositions; and, conversely, that known propositions are correlative with answered questions, since to know that p, one must be in a position cogently to provide a correct answer to the question: Is p the case?

To be sure, *answering* a question is not simply a matter of giving a response that happens to be correct. For a proper answer must not just be correct but also credible: it must have the backing of a rationale that renders its correctness evident. For example, take the question whether the mayor of San Antonio had eggs for breakfast yesterday. You say yes, I say no—though neither of us has a clue. One of us is bound to be right. But neither one of us has managed to provide an actual answer to the question. One of us has made a verbal response that happens to be correct, but neither of us has given a cognitively appropriate answer in the sense of the term that is now at issue. For doing so would require the backing of a cogent rationale of credibility; merely to guess at an answer, for example, or to draw it out of a hat, is not really to provide one.

For our purpose here we shall use Q, Q', Q'', and so on, as variables over questions; p, q, r, and so on, as variables ranging over propositions; x, y, z, and so on, as variables ranging over (actual) knowers; and a, b, c, and so on, over knowers in general (actual or possible). Kxp will represent "x knows that p." And we shall employ the following abbreviations with respect to questions:

$p \alpha Q$ iff p is a *possible* (meaningful) answer to Q.

For while "The Butler killed Sir John" may be the *correct* answer to the question, still "The Chauffeur killed Sir John" is a perfectly *meaningful* answer to it. On this basis we have it that the variables Q, and so on, range over meaningful questions, where a question is meaningful if and only if there is a meaningful possible answer to it. We, thus, have

$$(\forall Q)(\exists p)(p \alpha Q).$$

And since questions that have possible answers will also have actual (that is, *true* or *correct*) answers, we also have

$$(\forall Q)(\exists p)(p @ Q), \text{ where } p @ Q \text{ iff } p \ \& \ (p \alpha Q).$$

An @-answer is one that is not just possible but also actually correct.

As already indicated, to actually answer a question is *to know what the answer is,* and in this sense we have it that

x answers Q iff $(\exists p) Kx(p @ Q)$.

Moreover we further have

Q is an *answered* (or *resolved*) question if and only if someone answers it correctly: $(\exists p)(\exists x) Kx(p @ Q)$,

and

Q is an *answerable* (or *resolvable*) question if some possible knower has an answer to it, so that $(\exists p)(\exists a) Ka(p @ Q)$.

We shall here subscribe to a *metaphysical supposition* to the effect that some *possible* knower knows whatever is (possibly) knowable:

$\Diamond(\exists x) Kxp$ iff $(\exists a) Kap$

On this basis, Q is an answerable question if and only if it is possible for someone to answer it. (Thus, the variable Q ranges over all answerable questions, as already noted.)

Problematic Questions

Initially, the schoolmen understood by insolubilia such self-refuting propositions as that of the Liar Paradox ("What I am saying is false"). However, the term eventually came to cover a wider spectrum of examples, including all paradoxical situations in which the impracticability of seeing which side of the truth a matter lies on involves more than a mere lack of information.[1]

An instance is afforded by a yes/no question that cannot be answered correctly, such as "When you respond to this a question, will the answer be negative?" Consider the possibilities in display 1.

<table>
<tr><td colspan="2" align="center">DISPLAY 1
When next you answer a question, will the answer be negative?</td></tr>
<tr><td>Answer given</td><td>Truth status of the answer</td></tr>
<tr><td>Yes</td><td>False</td></tr>
<tr><td>No</td><td>False</td></tr>
</table>

On this basis, that query emerges as meaningless through representing a paradoxical question that cannot be answered correctly.

Another instance of a paradoxical question is "What is an example of a question you will never state (consider, conceive of)?" Any answer that you give is bound to be false, though *someone else* may well be in a position to give a correct answer. But paradoxical questions of this sort are readily generalized. Thus, consider "What is an example of a question no one will ever state (consider, conceive of)?" No one can answer this question appropriately. Yet, nevertheless, the question is not unanswerable in principle since there will certainly be questions that individuals and indeed knowers-at-large will never state (consider, conceive of). But it is impossible to give an example of this phenomenon. All such ill-formed questions will be excluded from our purview. Only meaningful questions that have correct answers will concern us here. (There are, of course, also questions that cannot be answered incorrectly. An instance is "What is an example of something that someone has given an example of?" Any *possible* answer to this question will be correct.)

Generic versus Specific Knowledge

Some questions are unanswerable for essentially practical reasons: we lack any prospect of finding effective means to resolve them, for reasons of contingent fact—the impracticability of time travel, say, or of space travel across the vast reaches involved. But such contingently grounded ignorance is not as bad as it gets. For some questions are in principle irresoluble in that purely theoretical reasons (rather than mere practical limitations) preclude the possibility of securing the information required for their resolution. There are—or may be—no sound reasons for dismissing such questions as meaningless, because we can readily imagine beings who can resolve them. But, given the inevitabilities of *our* situation as time-bound and finite intelligences, the questions may be such that any prospect of resolving them is precluded on grounds of general principle.

But are there any such questions? Are there some issues about which we are condemned to ignorance? There are two distinct possibilities for ignorance. One of them is general and nonspecific:

Generic question-resolving incapacity
    "There is some answerable question Q that I cannot answer":
    $(\exists Q)\sim(\exists p)Ki(p @ Q)$

The other mode of ignorance is particular and specific:

Specific question-resolving incapacity
    "Q is a particular answerable question that I cannot answer":
    $\sim(\exists p)Ki(p @ Q)$

This second situation, unlike the first, is a matter of concretely identifying the item at issue.

By the same token, there is a big difference between knowledge *that* (that there is an answer) and knowledge *what* (what the answer is), and thus between saying "Q has an answer and x does not know *that* this is so (that is, that Q has an answer),"
    $\sim Kx(\exists p)p @ Q,$

and saying "Q has an answer and x does not know *what* this answer is,
    $\sim(\exists p)Kx(p @ Q).$
On the other hand, consider the difference between
"Q has an answer and nobody knows what it is,"
    $(\exists p)(p @ Q) \& \sim(\exists x)(\exists p)Kx(p @ Q),$

and
"Q has an answer and nobody knows it (that is, that Q has an answer),
    $(\exists p)(p @ Q) \& \sim(\exists x)Kx(\exists p)(p @ Q).$

The latter of these is paradoxical in making an assertion that has the logical form of q & $\sim(\exists x)Kxq$ for a particular, definite proposition q. And while this can be *supposed*, it can never be seriously asserted, since a serious assertion is a claim to knowledge, and such a claim would, in the present context, issue in self-contradiction. On the other hand, the former of those two statements is perfectly coherent. There is no problem with the indefinite $(\exists q)(q$ & $\sim(\exists x)Kxq)$.

Intractability and Unanswerability

A tractable question is one that has a correct answer that could be provided by some intelligent being:

Q is *tractable* iff $(\exists p)[p @ Q$ & $\Diamond(\exists x)Kx(p @ Q)]$

In view of the aforementioned *metaphysical supposition*, this comes down to simply

$(\exists a)Ka(p @ Q)$.

Can a meaningful question prove to be intractable? Indeed, it can. For every finite knower there is some answerable question that this individual cannot answer—a question about the details of his own ignorance, for example. For as we have already insisted, whenever p is a fact that x does not know, then this circumstance, namely, that "p is a fact that x does not know," is something that x cannot know. We, thus, have

$(\forall x)(\exists\ Q)\sim(\exists p)Kx(p @ Q)$.

But now observe that if x cannot answer Q_1 and y cannot answer Q_2—where these are meaningful and thus answerable questions—then neither x nor y can answer the conjunctive question $Q_1 \wedge Q_2$. This means that we can move from the preceding to

$(\exists Q)(\forall x)\sim(\exists p)Kx(p @ Q)$.

Ordinarily, to be sure, one cannot move inferentially from $(\forall v)(\exists u)$ to $(\exists u)(\forall v)$. But in this special case of answering questions, this move is indeed possible. And this means that if there is always *for each sep-*

arate individual some questions that this individual cannot answer, then there must indeed be insolubilia: meaningful yet intractable questions that no one within a finite population of limited knowers is able to answer.

This state of affairs opens up the prospect that when we look at cognition from the angle of questions rather than of knowledge, then ignorance becomes concretely identifiable. As we have seen, it is impossible to give an instance of a truth that no one knows. But questions that no one can possibly answer correctly can indeed be found. It is instructive to pursue this prospect.

Unanswerable Questions

In inquiring into this problem area, we are not interested in questions whose unanswerability resides merely in the contingent fact that certain information is not in practice accessible. "Did Julius Caesar hear a dog bark on his thirtieth birthday?" Securing the needed information to answer this question is not possible here and now. (Time travel is still impracticable.) But, of course, such questions are not inherently unanswerable, and it is unanswerability as a matter of principle that will concern us here.[2]

There are two primary sorts of meaningfully unanswerable questions, those that are *locally* irresolvable, and those that are so *globally*. Locally unanswerable questions are those that a particular individual or group is unable to answer. An instance of such a question is "What is an example of a fact of which you are altogether ignorant?" Clearly you cannot possibly manage to answer this, because whatever you adduce as such a fact must be something you know or believe to be such (that is, a fact), so you cannot possibly be altogether ignorant of it. On the other hand, it is clear that *somebody else* could readily be in the position to answer the question. Again, consider such questions as

"What is an example of a problem that will never be considered by any human being?"
"What is an example of an idea that will never occur to any human being?"

There are sound reasons of general principle (the potential infinitude of problems and ideas; the inherent finitude of human intelligence) to hold that the items at issue in these questions (problems that will never be considered; ideas that will never occur) do actually exist. And it seems altogether plausible to think that other (nonhuman) hypothetically envisionable intelligences could well answer these questions correctly. But it is equally clear that we humans could never provide the requisite answers.

Looking beyond this we can also contemplate the prospect of globally intractable questions such that nobody (among finite intelligences, at least) can possibly be in a position to answer them (in the strict sense described at the outset). These questions have an appropriate answer, but for reasons of general principle no one—no finite intelligence, at least—can possibly be in a position to provide it. On this basis, Q is a globally intractable question if and only if

$$(\exists p)(p @ Q \ \& \sim(\exists p)(\exists x)\Diamond Kx[p @ Q]).$$

An example of such globally unanswerable questions can be provided by nontrivial but inherently uninstantiable predicates along the lines of

"What idea is there that has never occurred to anybody?"

"What occurrence is there that no one ever mentions?"

There undoubtedly are such items, but, of course, they cannot be instantiated, so questions that ask for examples here are inherently unanswerable.[3]

The questions that will concern us here are those that are both answer possessing and unanswerable; that is, they have answers, but these answers cannot be specified. Now answer possession comes to $(\exists p)(p @ Q)$. But if this answer were to be specified, we would then have it that *for some specific* p_0 it can be established that $p_0 @ Q$. And if we ourselves $(= i)$ could determine this, then we would have it that

$$Ki(p_0 @ Q).$$

And on this basis it would follow that

$$(\exists x)(\exists p)Kx(p @ Q).$$

But given the hypothesis of unanswerability it is just exactly this that cannot be. With answer-possessing but unanswerable questions it accordingly must transpire that the answer that, abstractly speaking, has to be there is one that cannot possibly be specified by way of particularized identification.

If such questions can indeed be adduced, then, though one cannot identify an *unknown* truth, one would be able to identify cases of *unspecifiable* truth, propositions such that either p_0 or not-p_0 must be true and yet nevertheless there is no prospect of determining which it is. Here, we can localize truth by emplacing it within a limited range (one, here, consisting of p_0 and $\sim p_0$) but cannot pinpoint it within this range of alternatives. One member of the assertion/denial pair will unquestionably prove to be true. So one way or the other, a case of truth stands before us. It is just that we cannot possibly say which member of the pair it is: the specifics of the matters are unknowable. But are there such unspecifiable truths?

17

Unknowable Truth

Intractable Questions About the Future and Surd Generalities

As already noted, we can move from the by-x unanswerability of "What is an example of truth that you, x, do not know to be so?" to the universally insoluble "What is an example of a truth that no one whatsoever knows to be so?" For in a finite society of imperfect knowers, the existence of such a truth is guaranteed by the conjunctivity principle mooted earlier, that if t_1 is a truth that x_1 does not know it to be so and t_2 is a truth that x_2 does not know to be so, then t_1 & t_2 is a truth neither knows to be so. But while we must suppose reality's complexity to be such that there are unknowable facts, we nevertheless cannot provide any specific examples of them. For, as already observed, the specification of unknowable facts is totally infeasible, since establishing factuality would automatically clash with unknowability. Knowledge being knowledge *of fact*, whatever instances of unknown truth that we can consider have to remain in the realm of conjecture rather than of knowledge. Given that knowledge fails us here, we must resort to guesswork. Accordingly, let us now explore the prospect of making an at least plausible conjecture at specifying an unknowable truth.

With cognitively finite beings knowing in general *that* every A is a B (knowing that every U.S. president is native born) does not mean knowing *of* every particular A that *it* is B (knowing specifically of every U.S. president—those of the future included—that he or she is native born), since, after all, one may not be able to identify those A's at all (to know who those future presidents will be). And so, in a setting of cognitive finitude, the fact that $Kx(\forall u)F(u)$ does not automatically entail $(\forall u)KxF(u)$ means that the former must be compatible with the *negation* of the latter: $(\exists u)\sim KxF(u)$. But when we assume that there is a u-value u_0 that validates the latter, so that $\sim KxF(u_0)$, then this contradicts $Kx(\forall u)F(u)$. So it is clear that $(\exists u)\sim KxF(u)$ is *not* going to be instantiable. Accordingly, giving concrete examples of unknowable truths is inherently infeasible.

On this basis, we have it that "unknowably true" is a *vagrant* predicate—one that has no determinate address in that it admits of no identifiable instance. Instantiating this sort of thing can only be done at the level of conjecture, not of knowledge. And this situation provides a window onto a larger scene.

Limits to Knowledge of the Future

Let us return in this light to the problem of our knowledge of the scientific future. Clearly, to identify an insoluble scientific problem we would have to show that a certain inherently appropriate scientific question is nevertheless such that its resolution lies beyond every (possible or imaginable) state of future science. This is obviously a *very* tall order—particularly so in view of our inevitably deficient grasp of future science. After all, the most evidently unknowable aspect of the future is invention, discovery, innovation—particularly in the case of science itself. As Immanuel Kant insisted, every new discovery opens the way to others, every question that is answered gives rise to yet further questions to be investigated.[1] The present state of science can never speak definitively for that of the future, since it cannot even predict what questions will be on the agenda.

After all, we cannot foresee what we cannot conceive of. Our questions—let alone answers—cannot outreach the limited horizons of our concepts. Having never contemplated electronic computing machines as such, the ancient Romans could also venture no predictions about their impact on the social and economic life of the twenty-first century. Clever though he unquestionably was, Aristotle could not have pondered the issues of quantum electrodynamics. The scientific questions of the future are, at least in part, bound to be conceptually inaccessible to the inquirers of the present. The question of just how the cognitive agenda of some future date will be constituted is clearly irresolvable for us now. Not only can we not anticipate future discoveries now; we cannot even pre-discern the questions that will arise as time moves on and cognitive progress with it.[2]

Scientific inquiry is a venture in innovation. And in consequence it lies in the nature of things that present science can never speak decisively for future science, and present science cannot predict the specific discoveries of future inquiry. After all, our knowledge of the present cannot encompass that of the future—if we could know about those future discoveries now, they would not have to await the future. Accordingly, knowledge about what science will achieve overall, and thus just where it will be going in the long run, are beyond the reach of attainable knowledge at this or any other particular stage of the scientific "state of the art."

It is clear on this basis that the question "Are there nondecidable scientific questions that scientific inquiry will never resolve, even were it to continue *ad infinitum*"—the insolubilia question, as we may call it—is one that cannot possibly ever be settled in a decisive way. After all, how could we possibly establish that a question Q about some issue of fact will continue to be *raisable and unanswerable* in every future state of science, seeing that we cannot now circumscribe the changes that science might undergo in the future? And, since this is so, we have it that this question itself is, quite interestingly, self-instantiating: it is a question regarding an aspect of reality (of which, of course, science itself is a part) that scientific inquiry will never, at any specific state of the art, be in a position to settle decisively.[3]

The long and short of it is that the very impredictability of future knowledge renders the identification of *insolubilia* impracticable. (In this regard it is effectively a bit of good future that we are ignorant about the lineaments of our ignorance.)[4] We are cognitively myopic with respect to future knowledge. It is in principle infeasible for us to tell now but only how future science will answer present questions but even what questions will figure on the question agenda of the future, let alone what answers they will engender. In this regard, as in others, it lies in the inevitable realities of our condition that the detailed nature of our ignorance is hidden by an impenetrable fog of obscurity.

Retrospect

As the survey of display 2 indicates, the present deliberations have carried us across a wide range of issues involving unanswerable questions.

DISPLAY 2
A survey of unanswerable questions

---

1. Pseudo-questions that admit of no correct answer
   - Paradoxical questions
   - Questions based on false presuppositions
2. Questions with correct answers that cannot be established due to contingent limits on accessible fact
   - Questions beset by circumstantially conditional information unavailability
3. Insolubilia: Questions that have correct answers that lie in principle beyond the reach of finite intelligences
   - Questions involving vagrant predicates
   - Questions involving randomness and chance (future contingency)
   - Questions involving cognitive innovation

So much, then, for unanswerable questions. But can one plausibly manage a transit from unanswerable questions to unknowable facts?

Intimations of Unknowable Truth

It is clear that the question
"What's an example of a truth one cannot establish as such—a fact that we cannot come to know?"

is one that leads *ad absurdum*. The quest for unknowable facts is inherently quixotic and paradoxical because of the inherent conflict between the definitive features at issue: factuality and unknowability. Here, we must abandon the demand for *knowledge* and settle for mere *conjecture*. But how far can we go in this direction?

To elucidate the prospect of identifying unknowable truth, let us consider the historicity of knowledge once more—in particular, a thesis on the order of

T. As long as scientific inquiry continues in our universe, there will always be a time when some of the then-unresolved (but resolvable) questions on the scientific agenda of the day will be sufficiently difficult as to remain unresolved for at least two years.

What is at issue here is clearly a matter of fact—one way or the other. But now let Q^* be the question "Is T true or not?" It is clear that to actually answer this question Q^* one way or the other we would need to have cognitive access to the question agenda of all future times. And, as emphasized earlier, in relation to theses of the $\forall\exists$ format just this sort of information about future knowledge is something that we cannot manage to achieve. By their very nature as such, the discoveries of the future are unavailable at present, and in consequence Q^* affords an example of an authentic insolubilium—a specific and perfectly meaningful question that we shall always and ever be unable to resolve decisively—irrespective of what the date on the calendar happens to be.

Yet, while the question admits of no definitive answer, it lies open to reasonable conjecture—something that is, of course, very far from achieving *knowledge*. And viewed in this light the thesis (*T*) is altogether plausible; it has all the earmarks of a likely truth.[5] And so it seems reasonable to hold that a conjecture of this sort is the best and most that we can ever hope to achieve, given that actual knowledge in such a matter is clearly unattainable.

18

Implications of Cognitive Limitation

The Scope of Ignorance

While there are, indeed, cognitive insolubilia—and we can plausibly identify some of them—the fact remains that detailed knowledge about the *extent* of our ignorance is unavailable to us. For what is at stake with this issue of extent is the size-ratio of the manifold of what one does know to the manifold of that what one does not. And getting a clear fix on the latter is not possible. For the actual situation is not a crossword puzzle or a geographic exploration where we can somehow measure the size of the terra incognita in advance. We can form no sensible estimate of the imponderable domain of what can be known but is not. That our knowledge is *pragmatically* sufficient for our immediate purposes—in enabling us to answer the questions that then and there confront us—is something that is in principle determinable. But that it is *theoretically* adequate to answer not just our present questions but also those that will grow out of them in the course of future inquiry is something we can never manage to establish. To be sure, we can compare what one person or group knows with what some other person or group knows. But mapping the realm of what is knowable is beyond our powers.

And so we return to one of the salient points of these deliberations:

the ironic, though in some ways fortunate, fact that we simply cannot make a reliable assessment of the extent and substance of our ignorance.

Realism

One of the most fundamental aspects of our concept of a real thing is that our knowledge of it is imperfect—that the reality of something actual, any bit of concrete existence, is such as to transcend what we can know, since there is always more to be said about it. And the inescapable fact of fallibilism and limitedness—of our absolute confidence that our putative knowledge does *not* do justice to the truth of the matter of what reality is actually like—is surely one of the best arguments for a realism. After all, the truth and nothing but the truth is one thing, but the *whole* truth is something else again. And if a comprehensively adequate grasp of "the way things really are" is beyond our powers, then this very circumstance itself constitutes a strong ground for a conviction that there is more to reality than we humans do or can know about.

In particular, the world's descriptive complexity is literally limitless. For it is clear that the number of true descriptive remarks that can be made about a thing—about any concrete element of existence, any particular physical object—is theoretically inexhaustible. Take a stone, for example. Consider its physical features: its shape, surface texture, chemistry. And then consider its causal background: its genesis and subsequent history. And then consider its functional aspects as reflected in its uses by the stonemason, the architect, the landscape designer. There is, in principle, no end to the different lines of consideration available to yield descriptive truths, so that the totality of potentially available facts about a thing—about any real thing whatsoever—is bottomless. John Maynard Keynes's so-called *principle of limited variety* is simply wrong: there is no inherent limit to the number of distinct descriptive kinds or categories to which the things of this world can belong. As best as we can possibly tell, natural reality has an infinite descriptive depth. It confronts us with a *law of natural complexity: There is no limit to the number of natural kinds to which any concrete particular belongs.*[1]

The cognitive intractability of things is accordingly something about which, in principle, we cannot delude ourselves, since such delusion would vindicate rather than deny a reality of facts independent of us. It is the very limitation of our knowledge of things—our recognition that reality extends beyond the horizons of what we can possibly know about it—that perhaps best betokens the mind-transcendence of the real. The very inadequacy of our knowledge militates toward philosophical realism because it clearly betokens that there is a reality out there that lies beyond the inadequate gropings of mind.

A Cognitively Indeterminate Universe

The past may be a different country, but the cognitive future is a terra incognita. Its entire cognitive landscape—its science, technology, intellectual fads and fashions—all lie outside our ken. We cannot begin to say what ideas will be at work here, though we know on general principles they will differ from our own. And whenever our ideas cannot penetrate, we are for that very reason impotent to make any detailed predictions.

Throughout the domain of inventive production in science, technology, and the arts we find processes of creative innovation whose features defy all prospects of predictability. The key fact in this connection is that of the fundamental epistemological law *the cognitive resources of an inferior (lower) state of the art cannot afford the means for foreseeing the operations of a superior (higher) one.* Those who know only tic-tac-toe cannot foresee how chess players will resolve their problems.

We know—or, at any rate, can safely predict—*that* future science will make major discoveries (both theoretical and observational/phenomenological) in the next century, but we cannot say *what* they are and *how* they will be made (since otherwise we could proceed to make them here and now).[2] We could not possibly predict now the substantive content of our future discoveries—those that result from our future cognitive choices—because to do so would be to transform them into present discoveries, which, by hypothesis, they just are not. In the context of questions about matters of scientific importance, then, we must be prepared for surprises.

It is a key fact of life that ongoing progress in scientific inquiry is a process of *conceptual* innovation that always places certain developments outside the cognitive horizons of earlier workers because the very concepts operative in their characterization become available only in the course of scientific discovery itself. (Short of learning our science from the ground up, Aristotle could have made nothing of modern genetics.) Newton could not have predicted findings in quantum theory any more than he could have predicted the outcome of American presidential elections. We cannot now predict the future states of scientific knowledge in detail because we do not yet have at our disposal the very concepts in which the issues will be posed.[3]

One important postscript: Our cognitive imperfection means that the universe itself is unpredictable. For a world in which as a matter of basic principle the future knowledge and thereby the future thoughts of intelligent beings are, at least in part, not predictable is one in which the correlative physical phenomena are unpredictable as well. For what intelligent beings do will always in some ways reflect the state of their knowledge, and where this is not predictable, so will their actions be. As long as intelligent agents continue to exist within the world and act therein under the guidance of their putative knowledge, the world is—and is bound to be—in part unpredictable. Making the world pervasively predictable would require the extinction of intelligent agents.[4] Of course, if our cognitive efforts stood outside and apart from nature, things might be different in this regard, since physical predictability might then be combined with a "merely epistemic" mental unpredictability. But this, clearly, is a prospect that is implausible in the extreme.

Appendix 1

A Survey of Thesis Acceptability

It is instructive to consider a round-up of the basic facts of modal epistemic logic as articulated in the preceding pages. The resulting thesis-acceptability situation is set out in table 1 (*x*-first spectra) and table 2 (*t*-first spectra). The theses at issue here can be an arrayed spectrum of groups of four related by the implication pattern:

As these tabulations indicate, the overarching rule here is that throughout all of these spectra *the mode of* t-*quantification is determinative for acceptability.* The ($\forall t$)-governed theses are uniformly unacceptable, and the ($\exists t$)-governed ones uniformly acceptable. The mode of *t*-quantification is thus determinative throughout. It would be difficult to find a more vivid illustration of the truism that it is risky to generalize about our knowledge of the truth.

TABLE 1   INITIAL-x THESES

(A)	I.	$(\forall x)(\forall t)\Diamond Kxt$	$-$	by AIII
	II.	$(\forall t)(\exists x)\,\Diamond Kxt$	$+$	from $(\forall x)(\exists t)Kxt$ (chapter 2)
	III.	$(\exists x)(\forall t)\,\Diamond Kxt$	$-$	chapter 10
	IV.	$(\exists x)(\exists t)\,\Diamond Kxt$	$-$	by AII
(B)	I.	$(\forall x)\Diamond(\forall t)Kxt$	$-$	by BIII
	II.	$(\forall x)\Diamond(\exists t)Kxt$	$+$	by AII
	III.	$(\exists x)\Diamond(\forall t)Kxt$	$-$	(chapter 9) also by CIII
	IV.	$(\exists x)\Diamond(\exists t)Kxt$	$+$	by AII
(C)	I.	$\Diamond(\forall x)(\forall t)Kxt$	$-$	by CIII
	II.	$\Diamond(\forall x)(\exists t)Kxt$	$+$	from FII
	III.	$\Diamond(\exists x)(\forall t)Kxt$	$-$	(chapters 9 and 12)
	IV.	$\Diamond(\exists x)(\exists t)Kxt$	$+$	by BII
(D)	I.	$(\forall x)(\forall t)\Box Kxt$	$-$	from $\sim(\forall x)(\forall t)Kxt$ (#2.5)
	II.	$(\forall x)(\exists t)\Box Kxt$	$+$	(chapter 9)
	III.	$(\exists x)(\forall t)\Box Kxt$	$-$	from $\sim(\exists x)(\forall t)Kxt$ (#2.5)
	IV.	$(\exists x)(\exists t)\Box Kxt$	$+$	by DII
(E)	I.	$(\forall x)\Box(\forall t)Kxt$	$-$	by DI
	II.	$(\forall x)\Box(\exists t)Kxt$	$+$	by FII
	III.	$(\exists x)\Box(\forall t)Kxt$	$-$	by DIII
	IV.	$(\exists x)\Box(\exists t)Kxt$	$+$	by EII
(F)	I.	$\Box(\forall x)(\forall t)Kxt$	$-$	by CI
	II.	$\Box(\forall x)(\exists t)Kxt$	$+$	from $\vdash (\forall x)(\exists t)Kxt$ (#2.5)
	III.	$\Box(\exists x)(\forall t)Kxt$	$-$	by CIII
	IV.	$\Box(\exists x)(\exists t)Kxt$	$+$	by FII

Note: With each spectrum I-II-III-IV the same patterns of validity obtain: $-\ +\ -\ +$ (with IV following from II in each case). The $(\forall t)$-governed theses are uniformly unacceptable and the $(\exists t)$-governed theses uniformly acceptable. The mode of t-quantification is thus determinative throughout.

TABLE 2   INITIAL-t THESES

With (A), (C), (D), and (E), only mixed cases need now be addressed: The x-first spectra of table 1 serve otherwise.

(A)	II	$(\forall t)(\exists x)\lozenge Kxt$	−	(chapters 11 and 12)
	III	$(\exists t)(\forall x)\,\lozenge Kxt$	+	by DIII
(B)	I	$(\forall t)\lozenge(\forall x)Kxt$	−	(chapter 11)
	II	$(\forall t)\lozenge(\exists x)Kxt$	−	(chapter 11)
	III	$(\exists t)\lozenge(\forall x)Kxt$	+	from $(\exists t)(\forall x)Kxt$ (chapter 2)
	IV	$(\exists t)\lozenge(\exists x)Kxt$	+	by BIII
(C)	II	$\lozenge(\forall t)(\exists x)Kxt$	−	(chapter 10)
	III	$\lozenge(\exists t)(\forall x)Kxt$	+	by FIII
(D)	II	$(\forall t)(\exists x)\square Kxt$	−	by AII
	III	$(\exists t)(\forall x)\square Kxt$	+	by EIII
(E)	I	$(\forall t)\square(\forall x)Kxt$	−	by BI
	II	$(\forall t)\square(\exists x)Kxt$	−	by BII
	III	$(\exists t)\square(\forall x)Kxt$	+	(chapter 9)
	IV	$(\exists t)\square(\exists x)Kxt$	+	by EIII
(F)	II	$\square(\forall t)(\exists x)Kxt$	−	by CII and EII
	III	$\square(\exists t)(\forall x)Kxt$	+	from $\vdash (\exists t)(\forall x)Kxt$ (chapter 2)

Note: With each spectrum I-II-III-IV the same pattern of validity obtains: − − + + (with IV following from III in each case). The $(\forall t)$-prefaced theses are uniformly unacceptable and the $(\exists t)$-prefaced ones uniformly acceptable. The mode of t-quantification is thus determinative throughout.

On Quantifying Knowledge (and the Gulf Between Linguistic Truth and Objective Fact)

How Much Can a Person Know? A Leibnizian Perspective on Human Finitude

How much can someone possibly know? What could reasonably be regarded as an upper limit of an individual's knowledge, supposing that factually informative knowledge rather than performative how-to knowledge is at issue? In pursuing this question, let us suppose someone with perfect recall who devotes a long lifespan to the acquisition of information. For 70 years this individual spends 365 days a year reading for 12 hours a day at the rate of 60 pages an hour (with 400 words a page). That yields a lifetime reading quota of some 7.4×10^9 words. Optimistically, supposing that, on average, a truth regarding matters of fact takes only some seven words to state; this means that our hypothetical person would have a lifetime access to 10^9 truths, all in all coming to a billion of them: 1,000,000,000. No doubt, most of us are a great deal less well informed than this. But it seems pretty well acceptable as an upper limit that the knowledge of a human individual could surely not reach and certainly not exceed.

After all, with an average of 400 words a page and 400 pages a book, this yields a total of 1.6×10^5 words a book, so that the previously indicated lifetime reading quota would come to some 4.6×10^y books. The world's largest libraries, the Library of Congress, for example, nowadays have somewhere around 20 million books (book-length assemblages of pamphlets included). It would take a truly Herculean effort to read through one-quarter of 1 percent of this library's vast collection. If mastery of Library of Congress–encompassed material is to be the measure, then few of us come within even 1 percent of that one-twentieth.[1] And this means that while a given individual can read *any* book (so that there are no *unreadable* books), the individual cannot possibly read *every* book (so that for anyone there are bound to be *unread* books).

This, of course, only addresses the question of how much a given person—one particular individual—can manage to know. There yet remains the question of how much is in principle knowable, that is, *can be known.* It is instructive to begin with the perspective of the great seventeenth-century polymath G. W. Leibniz, who, proceeding very much in the spirit of the preceding observations, wrote:

> All items of human knowledge can be expressed by the letters of the alphabet . . . so that it follows that one can calculate the number of truths of which humans are capable and thus compute the size of a work that would contain all possible human knowledge, and which would contain all that could ever be known, written, or invented, and more besides. For it would contain not only the truths, but also all the falsehoods that men can assert, and meaningless expressions as well.[2]

Thus, if one could set an upper limit to the volume of printed matter accessible to inquiring humans, then one could map out by combinatorial means the whole manifold of accessible verbal material—true, false, or gibberish—in just the manner that Leibniz contemplated. And this is exactly what he proceeded to do in a 1693 tract *De l'horizon de la doctrine humaine.*

Any alphabet devisable by man will have only a limited number of letters (Leibniz here supposes twenty-four). So even if we allow a word to become very long indeed (Leibniz supposes thirty-two letters) there will be only a limited number of words that can possibly be formed (namely 24 exp 32). So if we suppose a maximum to the number of words that a single intelligible statement can contain (say, one hundred), then there will be a limit to the number of potential "statements" that can possibly be made, namely 100 exp (24 exp 32).[3] The number, while huge, is nevertheless still finite, limited. And with an array of basic symbols different from those of the Latin alphabet the situation is changed in detail but not in structure. (And this remains the case even if one adds the symbols at work in mathematics, where Descartes' translation of geometrically pictorial propositions into algebraically articulated format stood before Leibniz's mind, to say nothing of his own project of a universal language and a *calculus ratiocinator*.[4])

The crux of Leibniz's discussion is that any known fact can in principle be spelled out in print. And there is only so much—so *finitely* much—that can be stated, and thereby also that can explicitly be thought. Moreover, this encompasses fiction as well—our knowledge of possibility is also finite, and fiction is for us just as much language-limited as the domain of truth. These considerations mean that as long as people manage their thinking in language—broadly understood to encompass diverse symbolic devices—the thoughts they can have, and *a fortiori* the things they possibly can know, will be limited in number.

Proceeding along these lines, let it be that the *cognitive* (in contrast to the *affective*) thought-life of people consists of the propositions that they consider. And now proceeding somewhat more realistically than above, let us suppose that people consider propositions at about the same speed at which they read, say one hundred pages an hour, with each page consisting of twenty sentences. Assuming a thought-span of sixteen waking hours on average, it will then transpire that in the course of a year a person entertains a number of thoughts equal to

$$365 \times 16 \times 100 \times 20 \cong 7 \times 10^6$$

So subject to the hypotheses at issue, this is how much material we would need to replicate the thought life of a person for an entire year. Once again, this number, though big, is nevertheless finite. There is only so much thinking that a person can manage. And these limits of language mean that there are only so many thoughts to go around—so many manageable sentences to be formulated. Once again, we are in the grip of finitude.

Statements Are Enumerable

When one construes the idea of an "alphabet" sufficiently broadly to include not only letters but also symbols of various sorts, it emerges that everything that can be stated in a language can be spelled out in print through the combinational combination of some finite register of symbols.[5] And with the conception of a "language" construed calling for development in the usual recursive manner, it transpires that the statements of a given language will be enumerable in number and can in theory be registered in one vast (unending) listing. Thus, if the languages at our disposal are finite in number—or, indeed, even if, while not finite, they are nevertheless enumerable—then the set of all statements (including every proposition that can possibly be formulated in the language) will be enumerably infinite.

We arrive accordingly at the following contention:

Thesis 1: *The enumerability of statements.* Statements (linguistically formulated propositions) are enumerable and thus (at most) denumerably infinite.

Truths Versus Facts

It serves the interests of clarity to introduce a distinction at this stage, that between truths and facts. Truths are linguistically articulated facts, correct statements formulated in language (broadly understood). A "truth" is something that has to be framed in *linguistic/symbolic* terms—the representation of a fact through its statement in some actual language, so that any correct statement in some actual language formulates a truth. (And the converse obtains as well: a *truth* must be encapsulated in a statement and cannot exist without linguistic embodiment.)

A "fact," on the other hand, is not a linguistic entity at all, but an actual circumstance that exists objectively in its own right, as an aspect of the world's state of affairs. Anything that is correctly statable in some (theoretically) *possible* language presents a fact.[6] Facts correspond to *potential* truths whose actualization hinges on an appropriate linguistic embodiment. Truths are statements and thereby language bound, but facts outrun our, or any, linguistic limits. Once stated, a fact yields a truth, but there may be no way to get from here to there. Truths state actual facts, they express those possible states of affairs that actually obtain. Facts, by contrast, are themselves those possible states of affairs that, if they were stated, would be truths. Truths involve a one-parameter possibilization: they encompass whatever can correctly be stated in some actual language. Facts, by contrast, involve a two-parameter possibilization, including whatever *can* be stated truly in some *possible* language. Truths are *actualistically* language-correlative, whereas facts are *possibilistically* language-correlative.[7]

Truths Though Infinite in Number Are Denumerable

Given that a denumerable infinity of statements can in principle be articulated in a language, and that either a statement or its negation will be true, it is only to be expected that a language will provide for a denumerable infinity of (contentually distinct) truths. After all, given that our ability to ask meaningful true-false (or yes-no) questions is unlimited, and that such questions are bound to have answers, there will be no limit to true assertions.[8] No matter how much is told to us on any conceivable topic regarding real things, we can ask for yet more pertinent information and in principle expect a correct answer. It is a crucial facet of our epistemic stance toward the real world that there is always more to be said than what we have so far managed. Every sector of reality has features lying beyond our present cognitive reach—at *any* "present" whatsoever. Reality's detail is such that more can always be said. No matter how many truths we may list in some finite series, at every step there will always be further truths whose content outreaches the information already provided within the series in question.

But, of course, any truth will be a linguistically formulated proposition. And this means that truths, though infinitely many, will be denumerable in number, given that linguistic statements can be enumerated. Accordingly we arrive at

Thesis 2: *The denumerability of truth.* Truths are denumerably infinite in number. The manifold of The Truth cannot be finitely inventoried.

The Inexhaustibility of Fact

Facts, too, are inexhaustible: the facts regarding any particular actual existent run off into endlessly proliferating detail. Moreover, every objective property of a real thing has consequences of a dispositional character, and these can never be intentioned *in toto*, because the dispositions that particular concrete things inevitably have endow them with an infinitistic aspect that cannot be comprehended within experience. This desk, for example, has a limitless manifold of phenomenal features of the type "having a certain appearance from a particular point of view." It is perfectly clear that most of these will never be actualized in experience. Moreover, to be a desk is to behave like a desk; to do what desks do. A thing *is* what it *does:* entity and lawful comportment are coordinated correlates, a good Kantian point. And this lawfulness means that the finitude of experience precludes any prospect of the *exhaustive* manifestation of the descriptive facets of any real things.[9]

And so we also arrive at

Thesis 3: *The inexhaustibility of fact.* Facts are infinite in number. The domain of fact is inexhaustible: there is no limit to facts about the real.

Reality Transcends the Descriptive Resources of Language

As these considerations suggest, reality outruns the descriptive resources of language: its complexity transcends the range of what language can take account of. Even if Wittgenstein was right in that the limits of language indeed are the limits of *our* world, they are nevertheless not the limits of *the* world.

The real in all its blooming buzzing activity is too rich for adequate representation by the recursive and enumerable resources of our language. We do and must recognize the limitations of our cognition, acknowledging that we cannot justifiably equate reality with what can, in principle, be known by us and thereby, in principle, be expressed in our language. And what is true here for the situation of our sort of mind is true for any other sort of finite mind as well. Any physically realizable sort of cognizing being can articulate, and thus can know, only a part or aspect of the real.

These deliberations lead us to

Thesis 4: The domain of fact is ampler than the domain of truths because language cannot capture the entirety of fact.

There is, as best as we can tell, no limit to the world's ever-increasing complexity that comes to view with our ever-increasing grasp of its detail. The realm of fact and reality is endlessly variegated and complex.

Facts Are Transdenumerable

While statements (and therefore true statements) can be enumerated, and truths are thus denumerable in number, there is no reason to suppose that the same will be true of facts. On the contrary, there is every reason to think that, reality being what it is, there will be an uncountably large manifold of facts.

There unquestionably are more facts, more states of affairs, than there are statements available for their formulation. For statements are linguistically formulated, and this means that the set of available statements, and statement complexes, is most countably infinite. But we live not in a digital world but an analogue one, so the manifold of its states of affairs, its configuration of fact, will, as will shortly appear, be transdenumerably infinite. And this, of course, means that there are more facts than truths, although it is obviously impossible to give a concrete example of this phenomenon. It follows that human knowledge, which consists in the cognitive grasp of truths, cannot possibly encompass the manifold of fact. Accordingly, it must be presumed that there are facts that we will never manage to formulate as truths, though it is obviously impossible to give concrete examples of this phenomenon.[10] "Unformulated fact" represents what might be termed a *vagrant* predicate—we cannot domicile it by way of instantiation at any specific spot. Though applicable in the abstract, it admits of no specifiable instance. (The idea of "a truth that nobody knows" affords another example.)

We thus arrive at the next principal thesis of these deliberations:

Thesis 5: *The transdenumerability of facts.* The manifold of fact is transdenumerably infinite.

Facts, unlike truths, cannot be enumerated, since no listing of truths—not even one of infinite length—can possibly manage to constitute a complete register of facts. For any attempt to register-fact-as-a-whole is bound to be incomplete, because there are facts about the list-as-a-whole that no single entry can encompass. The argument for the transdenumerability of fact can be developed as follows. Let us suppose (for the sake of *reductio ad absurdum* argumentation) that

$$f_1, f_2, f_3, \ldots$$

represents our (nonredundant but yet *complete*) listing of facts. Then, by the supposition of *factuality,* we have $(\forall i)f_i$. And, further, by the supposition of *completeness,* we have it that for all p:

(C) $(p \to (\exists i)[(f_i \to p)]$

Moreover, by the aforementioned supposition of *non-redundancy,* each member of the sequence adds something quite new to what has gone before.

   i. $(\forall j)[i < j \to \sim[(f_1 \& f_2 \& \ldots \& f_i) \to f_j)]$

Consider now the following course of reasoning:

1. $(\forall i)f_i$ by "factuality"
2. $(\forall j)f_j \to$ from (1) by "completeness" via the
   $(\exists i)(f_i \to (\forall j)f_j)$ substantiation of $(\forall j)f_j$ for p in (C)
3. $(\exists i)(f_i \to (\forall j)f_j)$ from (1), (2)

But (3) contradicts nonredundancy. This *reductio ad absurdum* of our hypothesis indicates that the facts about any sufficiently complex object will necessarily be too numerous for complete enumeration. In such circumstances, no purportedly comprehensive listing of truths can actually manage to encompass all facts.

The transdenumerability of fact yields the following:

Thesis 6. *There are quantitatively more facts than truths.* And in consequence, the manifold of Truth cannot accommodate the totality of the manifold of Fact.

Truths, being propositions formulated by the recursive resources of language, are denumerable. (Here language equals *actual* language, and these will be finite in number.) But facts will at most and at best correspond to potential truths, that is, possible truths statable in any of the potentially infinite array of *possible* languages. And there can, in principle, be an uncountable infinity of these. Every truth must state a fact, but given the limited resources of language, it is not only possible but indeed to be expected that there will be facts that elude stability in any actually available language and thereby fail to be captured as truths. (Again, it is obviously impossible to give a concrete illustration of this generality.) So, in the end, there are more facts than language can manage to capture.

What Does It Mean?

To clarify the situation here, it is helpful to consider an analogy, namely, that of integer-identification thought counting, where "counting" is to be a matter of indicating an integer by name—such as "thirteen" or "13"—rather than descriptively, such as "the first prime number after eleven."[11] Let us adopt an abbreviation. Let us suppose that there is a limit to the complexity of what people can know, so that, specifically, whenever comp $(p) > C$, then no one can manage to know that what proposition p claims is indeed so. Then there will, of course, be a class of (hypercomplex) truths that people cannot manage to know. But how does this "cannot" actually function?

With the ongoing development of cognitive sophistication in the course of human progress, who can say with rational assurance how far C can be increased. Indeed, for any specific quality n it is *possible* that C should eventually outstrip n:

$$(\forall n) \, \Diamond \, (C > n)$$

But, of course, C is always there as a limit. It is certainly *not* the case that
$$\Diamond(\forall n)(C > n),$$

so while it is possible for *any* fact to become known, nevertheless, what this does not imply, and what is emphatically *not* possible, is that *every* fact should become known. The difference in quantifier placement is crucial when one contemplates the prospect of unlimited knowability, of the idea that all facts are knowable.

Knowing facts is accordingly akin to counting integers in specifically the following way:

1. The manifold of integers is inexhaustible. We can never come to grips with all of them as specific individuals. In this regard, however,

2. Progress is always possible: we can always go beyond whatever point we have so far managed to reach. In principle we can always go further than we have already gone.

3. Moving forward gets ever more cumbersome. In moving onward we must be ever more prolix and make use of ever more elaborate symbol complexes. Greater demands in time, effort, and resources are inevitable here.

4. Thus, in actual practice there will be only so much that we can effectively manage to do. The possibilities that obtain in principle can never be fully realized in practice. However,

5. Such limitations in no way hamper the prospects of establishing various correct generalizations about the manifold of integers in its entirety.

Exactly the same sort of situation characterizes the cognitive condition of finite intelligences whose cognitive operations have to proceed by a symbolic process that functions by language. To begin with, inquiry, like counting, never achieves completeness. There is always more to be done: In both cases alike we can always manage to do more; in both cases we have no assurance that a generalization that obtains so far must continue to hold as the process continues, no guarantee that further items will not destabilize prevailing patterns. Moreover, in both cases there will be problems with approximation, since it cannot be said that what holds in the short run somehow approximates the long-range situation of the whole.

But does this not mean that those unknown facts are unknowable?

The answer is neither yes nor no. As already foreshadowed above, it all depends on exactly how one construes this matter of "knowability." Using *Kxf* to abbreviate "the individual X knows the fact *f*," there will clearly be two very different ways in which the existence of an unknowable fact can be claimed, namely,

$$(\exists f)\ \Box\ (\forall x) \sim Kxf$$

and

$$\Box(\exists f)(\forall x) \sim Kxf.$$

The second of these is, in the circumstances, inevitable, there being more facts than ever will or can be known. But the first is surely, or at least presumably, false. No *specific*, identifiable fact lies, in principle, outside the range of the knowable. (After all, to identify something *as a fact* is effectively to claim knowledge of it.)

Cognitive Limitations

Given that our explicit knowledge of fact is always mediated through language, it will be confined to truths. But just exactly what does all this mean for knowledge? What are we to make of the numerical disparity between facts and truths, between what is knowable in itself and what we can actually manage to know? It means, of course, that our knowledge is going to be incomplete. But just what does this portend?

Some writers analogize the cognitive exploration of the realm of fact to the geographic exploration of the earth. But this analogy is profoundly misleading. For the earth has a finite and measurable surface, and so even when there is unexplored terra incognita its magnitude and limits can be assessed in advance. Nothing like that obtains in the factual domain. The ratio and relationship of known truth to knowable fact is subject to no fixed (nonzero) proportion. Geographic exploration can expect eventual completeness; factual exploration cannot. There is no predetermined limit to the manifold of discoverable fact.

Language as we know it has a finite vocabulary. It puts only a finite (albeit, enlargeable) number of words at our disposal. And adjectives, and the distinctions and taxonomic differentiations they provide for, are finite in number. Nature, by contrast, is, as best as we can tell, a thing of infinite variety and variation. Its differences are subtle and admit of unending differentiation; it is not, as Keynes would have it, subject to a principle of limited variety. So in using a limited vocabulary to characterize an unending variable reality we oversimplify.

Induction with respect to the history of science itself—a constant series of errors of oversimplification—soon undermines our confidence that nature operates in the way we ourselves would deem the simplest. On the contrary, the history of science is an endlessly repetitive story of simple theories giving way to more complicated and sophisticated ones. The Greeks had four elements; in the nineteenth century Mendeleev had some sixty; by the 1900s this had gone to eighty, and nowadays we have a vast series of elemental stability states. Aristotle's cosmos had only spheres; Ptolemy's added epicycles; ours has a virtually endless proliferation of complex orbits that only supercomputers can approximate. Greek science was contained on a single shelf of books; that of the Newtonian age required a roomful; ours requires vast storage structures filled not only with books and journals but also with photographs, tapes, floppy disks, and the like. Of the quantities currently recognized as the fundamental constants of physics, only one was contemplated in Newton's physics: the universal gravitational constant. A second was added in the nineteenth century, Avogadro's constant. The remaining six are all creatures of twentieth-century physics: the speed of light (the velocity of electromagnetic radiation in free space), the elementary charge, the rest mass of the electron, the rest mass of the proton, Planck's constant, and Boltzmann's constant.[12] It would be naive, and quite wrong, to think that the course of scientific progress is one of increasing simplicity. The very reverse is the case: scientific progress is a matter of complexification, because over-simple theories invariably prove untenable in a complex world. The natural dialectic of scientific inquiry continuously impels us into ever deeper levels of sophistication.[13] In this regard our commitment to simplicity and systematicity, though methodologically necessary, is ontologically unavailing. For our more sophisticated researches invariably engender changes of mind, moving in the direction of an ever more complex picture of the world. Our methodological commitment to simplicity need not and will not preclude the substantive discovery of complexity.[14]

It follows from the preceding deliberations that we cannot possibly articulate, and thus come to know explicitly, "the whole story" about things. The domain of fact inevitably transcends the limits of our capacity to *express* it, and *a fortiori* those of our capacity to canvass it in overt detail. There are always bound to be more facts than we are able to capture in our linguistic terminology so that no language is capable of explicitly stating all facts.

At this point it seems sensible to return to the amazing discovery of the ancient Greeks that a handful of axioms can encompass an infinitude of theorems. Seemingly, it might be possible to have latent or implicit knowledge of an infinite domain through deductive systematization. Clearly, a finite set of axioms of a formal system can yield infinitely many theorems, and, indeed, a single general truth, such as $(\forall x)(x + 1 = 1 + x)$, where x ranges over the reals, will have a nondenumerable number of derivative consequences. So it might seem that, when we shift from overt or explicit to inferentially implicit knowledge, we secure the prospect of capturing a nondenumerably infinite manifold of fact as the knowledge content deductively implicit within a finite basis of explicit truth through recourse to axiomatic systematization.

But even here there are problems. For finite beings must deal in finite axiomatizations, and the reality of it is that if it is indeed the case that any attempt at a complete listing of truths is such that at every stage there will always be further facts that outrun the information already provided for inferentially by earlier members of the list, then the prospect of a (finite) axiomatization of the totality of truth is in principle blocked. After all, suppose that $f_1, f_2, \ldots, f_n$ afforded a finite axiomatizing of fact-as-a-whole, so that, whenever p is a fact, we would have

$$(f_1 \& f_2 \& \ldots \& f_n) \to p.$$

But now consider the following line of thought. Any given factual proposition *f* can only mention a finite number of individual items by their identifying name or index rather than by description. (See note 11.) And thus a finite number of such propositions can only deal with some finitely many specific particular individuals in this particularized manner. But there will certainly be various facts regarding more individuals than that which—for this very reason—cannot possibly be derived for from such a smaller basis.

We accordingly arrive at the following thesis:

Thesis 7. *The manifold of Truth-as-a-Whole* is not (finitely) axiomatizable and thereby not even tacitly knowable in its totality.

The long and short of it is that the factual domain is so vast that our reliance on the symbolic mechanisms of language precludes wrapping our thought around the whole of it.

Conclusion

Even though the actually achieved thought and knowledge of finite beings is destined to be ever finite, it nevertheless has no fixed and determinate limits. Return to our analogy. No matter how far out we go in counting integers, we can never get beyond the range of the finite. Even so with facts. There is a limit beyond which we *will* never get. But there is no limit beyond which we *can* never get. For the circumstance that there is always room for linguistic variation—for new symbols, new combinations, new ideas, new truths, and new knowledge—creates a potential for pushing our thought ever further.

Any adequate account of inquiry must accordingly recognize that the ongoing process of information acquisition at issue in science is a process of *conceptual* innovation. Caesar did not know—and in the then extant state of the cognitive art could not have known—that his sword contained tungsten and carbon. There will always be facts about a thing that we do not *know* because we cannot even *express* of them in the prevailing conceptual order of things. To grasp such a fact means taking a perspective of consideration that as yet we simply do not have, since the state of knowledge (or purported knowledge) has not reached a point at which such a consideration is feasible. The progress of science leaves various facts about the things of this world wholly outside the cognitive range of the inquirers of any particular period. Even though the thought of finite beings is destined ever to be finite, it nevertheless has no fixed and determinable limits.

The line of thought operative in these deliberations was already mooted by Kant:

> In natural philosophy, human reason admits of *limits* ("excluding limits," *Schranken*) but not of *boundaries* ("terminating limits," *Grenzen*), namely, it admits that something indeed lies without it, at which it can never arrive, but not that it will at any point find completion in its internal progress. . . . [T]he possibility of new discoveries is infinite: and the same is the case with the discovery of new properties of nature, of new powers and laws by continued experience and its rational combination.[15]

And here Kant was right—even on the Leibnizian principles considered at the outset of this discussion. The cognitive range of finite beings is indeed limited. But it is also boundless, because it is not limited in a way that blocks the prospect of cognitive access to ever new and continually different facts thereby affording an ever ampler and ever more adequate account of reality.[16]

Notes

CHAPTER 1: SETTING THE STAGE

1. Practical, how-to knowledge such as knowing how to bake doughnuts is left as a matter for action theory rather than logic. (Compare this with chapter 7.)

2. See Rudolf Carnap, *Meaning and Necessity* (Chicago, IL: University of Chicago Press, 1947; 2nd ed. 1956).

3. "Logiki wielowartościowe a formalizacje funkcji intensyonalnych" [Many-Valued Logics and the Formalization of Intensional Functions], *Kwartalnik filozoficzny* 17 (1948): 59–87. I know the contents of this paper only from the brief report by A. N. Prior in his *Formal Logic* (Oxford: Clarendon Press, 1955), 313; and from two reviews, the first by H. Hiż in *Mathematical Review* 10 (1949): 1–2; and the other by R. Suszko in *Journal of Symbolic Logic* 14 (1949): 64–65.

4. See the author's *The Limits of Science,* rev. ed. (Pittsburgh, PA: University of Pittsburgh Press, 1999).

5. See G. E. Moore, *Philosophical Studies* (London: Reoutledge & Kegan Paul, 1922).

6. Perhaps here the universal quantifier ∀ should be changed to the plurality quantifier M. On this quantifier, initially proposed by the author in 1965, see David Kaplan, "Rescher's Plurality Quantification," *Journal of Symbolic Logic* 31 (1966): 153–55.

7. On these issues see Jason Stanley and Timothy Williamson, "Knowing How," *Journal of Philosophy* 98 (2002): 411–44. See also Stephen Schiffer, "Amazing Knowledge," *Journal of Philosophy,* 99 (2002).

CHAPTER 2: BASIC PRINCIPLES

1. While s is not a proper knower as such, we have it that Ksp entails $(\exists x)Kxp$, seeing that one would not introduce into K something that one does not accept as a known truth.

2. The difficulties arising here are generally discussed under the heading the "lottery paradox." For the literature on this subject see H. K. Kyburg Jr., *Probability and the Logic of Rationale Relief* (Middletown, CT, 1961); Kyburg, "Conjunctivitis" in *Induction, Acceptance, and Rational Belief,* ed. M. Swain (Dordrecht: Rei-

del, 1970); I. Levi, *Gambling with Truth* (New York: Knopf, 1967); R. Hilpinen, *Rules of Acceptance and Inductive Logic* (Amsterdam, 1968) and (D. Reidel, 1970); and Alan Goldman, "A Note on the Conjunctivity of Knowledge," *Analysis* 3 (1975).

    3. See appendix 1.

CHAPTER 3: DEDUCTIVITY AND KNOWLEDGE AMPLIATION

    1. Unrealistic though K^* is as a construal of knowledge, it is very much in favor among logicians, most of whom take this sort of knowledge as standard. On this issue, see Ronald Fagin, Joseph Y. Halpern, Yoram Moses, and Moshe Y. Vardi, *Reasoning About Knowledge* (Cambridge, MA: MIT Press, 1995), especially chaps. 3 and 9.

    2. The existence of such secrets will be discussed in chapters 4 and 10.

CHAPTER 4: METAKNOWLEDGE

    1. For further detail regarding the *KK* thesis, see Roy A. Sorensen, *Blindspots* (Oxford: Clarendon Press, 1988), esp. 117–59, 239–46, 289–92, and 312–20.

CHAPTER 5: FOR AUGHT THAT SOMEONE KNOWS

    1. The "knows" in "for aught that x knows" is here taken strictly and literally. So even when x does not *know* that not-*p*, this still leaves open the possibility that x has pretty strong evidence for it.

CHAPTER 6: GROUP KNOWLEDGE

    1. The situation here is fundamentally analogous to physical collaboration along the lines "Tom and Bob and Ted carried the bookshelf upstairs" (as contrasted with, say, the three of them taking up the books that were on the shelf). On these issues, see G. M. Massey, "Tom, Dick, and Harry, and All the King's Men," *American Philosophical Quarterly* 13 (1976): 89–107.

    2. An informative treatment of cooperation in general, without, however, any specific reference to inquiry or research, can be found in Raimo Tuomela, *Cooperation: A Philosophical Study* (Dordrecht: Kluwer Academic Publishers, 2000).

CHAPTER 7: PROPOSITIONAL VERSUS INTERROGATIVE KNOWLEDGE

    1. In fact, we have been doing just this sort of "quantifying-in" since introducing the "for aught that x knows" (Axp) operator in chapter 5.

    2. The situation would, of course, change if we had $Kx(Fu \vdash Gu)$, for the inference would now hold.

CHAPTER 8: COLLECTIVE VERSUS DISTRIBUTIVE KNOWLEDGE AND KNOWER LIMITEDNESS

1. To say that x knows what the S members are and also that each of them has F would require that

$$(\forall u)(u \in S \supset Kx[u \in S \& Fu]).$$

Observe further that

$$(\forall u)(u \in S \supset KxFu)$$

says something quite different from any of the previous statements. For now, the concept of S-membership does not—or need not—figure at all in the scope of x's knowledge. The very idea of S-membership need never have occurred to x for this thesis to be true. Thus, while collective knowledge is *de dicto* knowledge of a universal fact that obtains universally regarding some group, the presently contemplated sort of knowledge is extensionally individualized *de re* knowledge regarding the sundry individuals that comprise that group. And this is another story altogether.

2. Note that neither of the two preceding statements comes to

$$(\exists u)(u \& s \& KxFu).$$

Here, x merely knows that something has F, which happens (possibly unbeknownst to x) to be an S-member. As far as x's knowledge is concerned, S-membership remains altogether out of the picture.

3. This line of thought will be developed further in chapter 14.

4. Such knower limitedness is something different from the knower finitude at issue with the incapacity to achieve knowledge of the form

$$(\forall u) \, KxFu,$$

with respect to any infinite $\forall$-range of items.

5. To be sure, one can know of some particular truth that one does not know it; it is just that one cannot concurrently realize its status as a truth.

6. On blind spots, see Sorensen *Blindspots*.

7. Further attention will be devoted to these issues in chapters 17 and 18.

CHAPTER 9: MODALITY

1. The converse of this first principle,

$$(\forall u)\Box Fu \supset \Box(\forall u)Fu,$$

does not obtain in the context of the present deliberations. For an absolute (unmodalized) quantifier ranges over all *existing* individuals, whereas a modalized quantifier ranges over *possible* individuals. And even if all actual individuals are necessarily *F*s, it does not follow that necessarily all *possible* individuals will be *F*s.

2. But why not also have the thesis that

$$\Diamond(\forall u)Fu \vdash (\forall u)\Diamond Fu?$$

Because it is equivalent with

$$(\exists u)\Box Fu \vdash \Box(\exists u)Fu.$$

And this is untenable. For although there in fact exists something (Grant's tomb) that necessarily memorializes Ulysses S. Grant, this does not entail that the existence of something that memorializes Grant is necessary. Moreover, it is clear that we do not have the converse thesis

$$\Box(\exists u)Fu \vdash (\exists u)\Box \ Fu \text{ or equivalently } (\forall u)\Diamond Fu \vdash \Diamond(\forall u)Fu.$$

Because it is necessary that there is some integer that counts the number of people in the room, it does not follow that the number of people in the room (whatever it may be) is so necessarily.

3. This line of thought also blocks the path to

$$(\forall u)\Box Fa \supset \Box(\forall u)Fu.$$

4. For example, this tendency is pushed to extreme and distinctly implausible lengths in Fagin et al. *Reasoning About Knowledge.*

Chapter 12: Unknowability

1. This terrain at large is canvassed in several recent books, including the author's *The Strife of Systems* (Pittsburgh, PA: University of Pittsburgh Press, 1985); and Timothy Williamson, *Knowledge and Its Limits* (Oxford: Oxford University Press, 2000): 270–301.

2. Frederic B. Fitch, "A Logical Analysis of Some Value Concepts," *Journal of Symbolic Logic* 28 (1963): 135–42.

3. W. D. Hart, "The Epistemology of Abstract Objects," *Proceedings of the Aristotelian Society* 53 (1979): 53–65.

4. Note that the structurally cognate thesis

$$\Diamond(\forall t)(\forall x)Kxt \text{ or equivalently } \Diamond(\forall x)(\forall t)Kxt,$$

to the effect that possibly everyone is omniscient, is ruled out by our focus on finite knowers. And its weaker cousin $\Diamond(\forall t)(\exists x)Kxt$ maintaining the possibility that every truth known by someone or other can also be ruled out. For since every member of our finite population of knowers has a secret, the *conjunction* of all of these is a proposition that it is not possible for anyone to know.

5. J. J. MacIntosh, "Fitch's Features," *Analysis* 44 (1984): 153–58.

6. Since we suppose that F is (as a *propositional* qualifier) closed under logical equivalence, then $Fp \supset p$ is equivalent with $p \supset \sim F\sim p$, and thesis (V) comes to $(\forall t)\sim F\sim t$. And, of course, (P) comes to $(\forall t)\Diamond Ft$.

CHAPTER 13: FITCH'S THEOREM AND ITS CONSEQUENCES

1. Let it be that x is the only person ever in a position to learn a certain fact—say, by being "the last man on earth"—but that his attention is otherwise engaged.

2. On this issue, see Sorensen, *Blindspots,* and Daniels, *Analysis.*

3. For the relevant literature, see the bibliography.

4. The individuals at issue in the "grand conjunction" t^* above will include us among the pertinent knowers, thereby automatically rendering t^* unspecifiable for us. We can know that something of this sort exists but cannot identify it. (Conjecture, of course, would be something else again.) On this issue with its emphasis on the difference between an individuating reference and an actual identification, see chapters 7, 16, and 17.

CHAPTER 14: FINITE AND INFINITE KNOWERS

1. To be sure, the prospect of inductively secured knowledge of laws is a philosophically controversial issue. But this is not the place to pursue it. (For the author's view of the matter, see his *Induction* (Oxford: Blackwell, 1980).

CHAPTER 15: VAGRANT PREDICATES AND NONINSTANTIABILITY

I am grateful to Philip Ehrlich for constructive comments on an early draft of this discussion of vagrant predicates.

1. We can, of course, refer to such individuals and even to some extent describe them. But what we cannot do is *identify* them in the sense specified in chapter 7.

2. A uniquely characterizing description on the order of "the tallest person in the room" will single out a particular individual without specifically identifying the person.

3. To be sure, one could (truthfully) say something like "The individual who prepared Caesar's breakfast on the fatal Ides of March is now totally unknown." But the person at issue here is indeed unknown—that is, he or she is alluded to but not specified, individuated but not concretely identified. So I cannot appropriately claim to know *who* the individual at issue is but only at best *that* a certain individual is at issue. (On this topic, see chapter 7.)

4. It is, of course, crucially different from

$(\exists u)(\exists x)Kx(Fu \ \& \ \sim\Diamond(\exists y)KyFu)$.

Here, as elsewhere, the position of the K operator relative to the environing quantifiers is crucial.

5. The thesis "I know that p is a known fact that I do not know" comes to

$Ki[(\exists x)Kxp \ \& \sim Kip])$ (here, i = oneself).

This thesis entails my knowing both $(\exists x)Kxp$ and $\sim Kip$. But the former circumstance entails Kip, and this engenders a contradiction. Of course, "knowing a certain particular fact" involves not just knowing *that there is* a fact, but also calls for knowing *what that fact is*.

6. Accordingly, there is no problem about "t_o is a truth *you* do not know," although I could not then go on to claim modestly that "You know everything that I do." For the contentions $\sim Kyt_o$ and $(\forall t)(Kit \supset Kyt)$ combine to yield $\sim Kit_o$, which conflicts with the claim Kit_o that I stake in claiming t_o as a truth.

CHAPTER 16: UNANSWERABLE QUESTIONS AND INSOLUBILIA

1. See Paul Vincent Spade, "Insolubilia," in *The Cambridge History of Later Medieval Philosophy,* ed. Norman Kretzmann et al. (Cambridge: Cambridge University Press, 1982), 246–53.

2. Nor will we be concerned here with the issue of indemonstrable truths and unanswerable questions in mathematics. Our concern is only with *factual* truths; the issue of truth in such formal descriptions as mathematics or logic will be left aside.

3. This issue here is one of so-called vagrant predicates that have no known address.

CHAPTER 17: UNKNOWABLE TRUTH

1. On this theme, see the author's *Kant and the Reach of Reason: Studies in Kant's Theory of Rational Systematization* (Cambridge: Cambridge University Press, 2000).

2. Of course, these questions already exist—what lies in the future is not their existence but their presence on the agenda of active concern.

3. And this issue cannot be settled by supposing a mad scientist who explodes the superbomb that blows the earth to smithereens and extinguishes all organic life as we know it. For the prospect cannot be precluded that intelligent life will evolve elsewhere. And even if we contemplate the prospect of a "big crunch" reversal of the "big bang," imploding our universe into punctiform compactness, the project can never be precluded that at the other end of the big crunch, so to speak, another era of cosmic development awaits.

4. That contingent future development is by nature cognitively intractable, even for God, was a prospect supported even by some of the scholastics. On this issue, see Marilyn McCord Adams, *William Ockham,* vol. 2 (Notre Dame, IN: University of Notre Dame Press, 1987), chap. 27.

5. And, of course, there are many other plausible theses of this sort, such as "As long as scientific inquiry continues in the universe, every scientific discovery will eventually be improved upon and refined."

CHAPTER 18: IMPLICATIONS OF COGNITIVE LIMITATION
1. For further detail on these issues, see the author's *Complexity* (New Brunswick, NJ: Transaction Publishers, 1998).
2. Recall the instructive anecdote of the musician who answered the question "Where is jazz heading" with the response "If I knew that, I'd be there already."
3. For further detail on these issues, see the author's *Limits of Science*.
4. To be sure, there doubtless are other sources of unpredictability in nature, apart from the doings of intelligent agents.

APPENDIX 2: ON QUANTIFYING KNOWLEDGE
1. To be sure, there lurks in the background the question of whether having mere *information* counts as having *knowledge*. With regard to this quantitative issue it has been argued that authentic knowledge does not increase propositionally with the amount of information as such, but only proportionally with its logarithm. See chap. 13 of the author's *Epistemology* (Albany, NY: SUNY Press, 2003). This would suggest that the actual knowledge within the Library of Congress's many volumes might be encompassed in some far more modest collection. But this sort of complication can be put aside as irrelevant to the course of reflection that will be unfolded.
2. Philip Beeley, ed., "Leibniz on the Limits of Human Knowledge," *Leibniz Review* 13 (December 2003): 95. On the larger context, see G. W. Leibniz, *De l'horizon de la doctrine humaine,* ed. Michael Fichant (Paris: Vrin, 1991).
3. G. W. Leibniz, *De l'horizon,* 11. This, of course, long antedates the (possibly apocryphal) story about the Huxley-Wilberforce debate, which has Huxley arguing that sensible meaning could result from chance process because a team of monkeys typing at random would eventually produce the works of Shakespeare—or (on some account) all the books in the British Library, including not only Shakespeare's works but the Bible as well. (The story, which goes back, at least, to Sir Arthur Eddington's *The Nature of the Physical World* [London: McMillan, 1929, 72–73], is doubtless fictitious, since the Huxley-Wilberforce debate of 1860 antedated the emergence of the typewriter.) However, the basic idea goes back at least to Cicero: "If a countless number of the twenty-one letters of the alphabet . . . were mixed together, it is possible that when cast on the ground they should make up the *Annals* of Ennius, able to be read in good order" (*De natura deorum,* II, 27).
4. Louis Couturat, *La logique de Leibniz* (Paris: Alcan, 1901) is still the best overall account of this Leibnizian project.
5. Compare Philip Hugly and Charles Sayward, "Can a Language Have Indenumerably Many Expressions?" *History and Philosophy of Logic* 4 (1983): 188–222.
6. Our position thus takes no issue with P. F. Strawson's precept that "facts are what statements (when true) state." Strawson, "Truth," *Proceedings of the Aris-*

totelian Society 24 (1950): 136. Difficulty would ensue with Strawson's thesis only if an "only" were added.

7. But can any sense be made of the idea of *merely* possible (that is, possible but nonactual) languages? Of course, it can! Once we have a generalized conception (or definition) of a certain kind of thing—be it a language or a caterpillar—then we are inevitably in a position to suppose that in the *de dicto* mode the possible actuality of things meeting these conditions are over and above those that in fact do so.

8. Complications regarding the principle of excluded middle are irrelevant for the present concerns.

9. This aspect of objectivity was justly stressed in the "second analogy" of Kant's *Critique of Pure Reason,* though his discussion rests on ideas already contemplated by Leibniz, *Philosophische Schriften,* vol. 7, ed. C. I. Gerhardt (Berlin, 1890), 319 ff.

10. Note, however, that if a Davidsonian translation argument to the effect that "if it is sayable at all, then it is sayable in *our* language" were to succeed—which it does not—then the matter would stand on a very different footing. For it would then follow that any possible language can state no more than what can be stated in our own (actual) language. And then the realm of facts—that is, what is (correctly) statable in some *possible* language—and the realm of truths—that is, what is (correctly) statable in some *actual* language—would necessarily coincide. Accordingly, our thesis that the range of facts is larger than the range of truths hinges crucially on a failure of such a translation argument. See Donald Davidson, "The Very Ideas of a Conceptual Scheme" (*Proceedings and Addresses of the American Philosophical Association* 47 (1973–1974): 5–20; see also the critique of Davidson's position in the author's *Empirical Inquiry* (Totowa, NJ.: Rowman & Littlefield, 1982), chap. 2.

11. And it does so by *naming* the number at issue rather than merely *describing* it. This distinction between understanding numbers *by name* and doing so *by description* is crucial for resolving Richard's "paradox," which results from such specifications as, for example, "the largest number one can identify with fewer than one hundred symbols" has in fact been identified with a good many fewer. Richard's analysis "Les principes de la mathématique et la problème des ensembles" was originally published in *Révue générale des sciences pures et appliquées* in 1905. It is translated in J. Hiejenoort, *Mathematical Logic* (Amsterdam: North Holland, 1967), 143–44. For a detailed discussion of this issue, see Alonzo Church, "The Richard Paradox," *American Mathematical Monthly* 61 (1934): 356–61.

12. See B. W. Petley, *The Fundamental Physical Constants and the Frontiers of Measurement* (Boston: Hilger, 1985).

13. On the structure of dialectical reasoning, see the author's *Dialectics* (Albany, NY: SUNY Press, 1977); for the analogous role of such reasoning in philosophy, see his *The Strife of Systems* .

14. For further ramifications of this line of thought, see the author's *Complexity*.

15. *Prolegomena to Any Future Metaphysics,* sec. 57. Compare the following passage from Charles Sanders Peirce: "For my part, I cannot admit the proposition of Kant—that there are certain impassable bounds to human knowledge. . . . The history of science affords illustrations enough of the folly of saying that this, that, or the other can never be found out. Auguste Comte said that it was clearly impossible for man ever to learn anything of the chemical constitution of the fixed stars, but before his book had reached its readers the discovery which he had announced as impossible had been made. Legendre said of a certain proposition in the theory of numbers that, while it appeared to be true, it was most likely beyond the powers of the human mind to prove it; yet the next writer on the subject gave six independent demonstrations of the theorem." Pierce, *Collected Papers,* 2nd ed. (Cambridge, MA: Harvard University Press, 1931–58), 6:6.556.

16. This discussion has profited from the constructive comments of several colleagues at the University of Pittsburgh, including Jason Dickinson, Mickey Perloff, and Laura Ruetsche.

Bibliography

Almog, Joseph. "Naming Without Necessity." *Journal of Philosophy* 83 (1986): 210–42.

Barcan Marcus, Ruth. "Modalities and Intensional Languages." *Syntheses* 13 (1961): 303–22.

Beall, J. C. "Fitch's Proof, Verificationism, and the Knower Paradox." *Australasian Journal of Philosophy* 78 (2000): 241–47.

Boh, Ivan. *Epistemic Logic in the Middle Ages.* London: Routledge, 1993.

Carnap, Rudolf. *Meaning and Necessity* (Chicago, IL: University of Chicago Press, 1947; enlarged ed. 1956; rev. ed. 1988).

Church, Alonzo. "On Carnap's Analysis of Statements of Assertion and Belief." *Analysis* 10 (1950): 97–99.

———. "Intensional Isomorphism and Identity of Belief." *Philosophical Studies* 5 (1954): 65–73.

Cohen, L. J. "Can the Logic of Indirect Discourse Be Formalized?" *Journal of Symbolic Logic* 22 (1957): 225–32.

Cohen, L. J., and A. C. Lloyd "Assertion Statements." *Analysis* 15 (1955): 66–70.

Daniels, C. B. "Privacy and Verification." *Analysis* 48 (1988): 100–102.

Davidson, Donald "Knowing One's Own Mind." *Proceedings and Addresses of the American Philosophical Association* vol. 60 (1987): 441–58.

Edgington, Dorothy. "The Paradox of Knowability." *Mind* 94 (1985): 557–68.

Ellis, Brian. *Rational Belief Systems.* Totowa, NJ: Rowman and Littlefield, 1979.

Evans, Gareth. *The Varieties of Reference.* Oxford: Clarendon Press, 1982.

Evans, M. G. J., and J. H. McDowell, eds. *Truth and Meaning.* Oxford: Oxford University Press, 1976.

Fagin, Ronald, Joseph Y. Halpern, Yoram Moses, and Moshe Y. Vardi. *Reasoning About Knowledge.* Cambridge MA: MIT Press, 1995.

Fine, Kit. "The Problem of de re Modality." In *Themes for Kaplan,* edited by J. Almog, R. Perry, and J. Wettstein. Oxford: Oxford University Press, 1989): 197–272.

Fitch, Frederic B. "A Logical Analysis of Some Value Concepts." *Journal of Symbolic Logic* 28 (1963): 135–42.

Forbes, Graeme. *Languages of Possibility*. Oxford: Basil Blackwell, 1989.

Girle, Rod. *Modal Logics and Philosophy*. Teddington, UK: Acumen, 2000.

Goldman, Alan. "A Note on the Conjunctivity of Knowledge." *Analysis* 3 (1975).

Goodstein, R. L. "On the Formalization of Indirect Discourse." *Journal of Symbolic Logic* 23 (1958): 417–19.

Hardin, Russell. *Collective Action*. Baltimore, MD: Johns Hopkins University Press, 1982.

Hart, W. D. "The Epistemology of Abstract Objects." *Proceedings of the Aristotelian Society* 53 (1979): 53–65.

Hilpinen, R. *Rules of Acceptance and Inductive Logic*. Amsterdam, 1968; *Acta Philosophica Fennica* 22.

Hintikka, Jaakko. *Knowledge and Belief*. Ithaca, NY: Cornell University Press, 1962.

Hintikka, Jaakko, and B. Merill. *The Logic of Epistemology and the Epistemology of Logic*. Dordrecht: Kluwer, 1989.

Hodes, Harold. "Axioms for Actuality." *Journal of Philosophical Logic* 4 (1984): 27–34.

Humberstone, I. L. "The Formalities of Collective Omniscience." *Philosophical Studies* 48 (1985): 401–23.

Jacquette, Dale. *A Companion to Philosophical Logic*. Oxford: Blackwell, 2002.

Jacquette, Dale, ed. *A Handbook of Philosophical Logic*. Amsterdam: Elsevier, forthcoming.

Kripke, Saul. *Naming and Necessity*. Cambridge, MA: Harvard University Press, 1980.

Kyburg, H. K. Jr. *Probability and the Logic of Rationale Relief*. Middletown, CT: University of Connecticut Press, 1961.

———. "The Rule of Detachment in Inductive Logic." In *The Problem of Inductive Logic*, edited by I. Lakatos, 98–119. Amsterdam: Reidel, 1968.

———. "Conjunctivitis." In *Induction, Acceptance, and Rational Belief*, edited by M. Swain. Dordrecht: Reidel, 1970.

Lehrer, Keith, and Carl Wagner. *Rational Consensus in Science and Society*. Dordrecht: D. Reidel, 1981.

Lenzen, Wolfgang. "Recent Work in Epistemic Logic." *Acta Philosophica Fennica* 30, no. 1 (1978), 199–233.

Levi, I. *Gambling with Truth*. New York: Knopf, 1967.

Linsky, Leonard. "On Interpreting Doxastic Logic." *Journal of Philosophy* 65 (1968): 500–502.

Łoś, Jerzy. "Logic wielowartościowe a formalizacje funkcji intensyonalnych" [Many-valued logics and the formalization of intensional functions]. *Kwartalnik filozoficzny* 17 (1948): 59–87.

MacIntosh, J. J. "Fitch's Features." *Analysis* 44 (1984): 153–58.

Massey, G. M. "Tom, Dick, and Harry, and All the King's Men." *American Philosophical Quarterly* 13 (1976): 89–107.

Moore, G. E. *Philosophical Studies.* London: Routledge & Kegan Paul, 1922.
———. *Some Main Problems of Philosophy.* London: Allen & Unwin, 1953.
Percival, Philip. "Fitch and Intuitionistic Knowability." *Analysis* 50 (1990): 182–87.
———. "Knowability, Actuality, and the Metaphysics of Context-Dependent." *Australasian Journal of Philosophy* 69 (1991): 82–97.
Priest, Graham. *In Contradiction: A Study of the Transconsistent.* The Hague: Martinus Nijhoff, 1987.
Priest, Graham, and Richard Sylvan. "The Philosophical Significance and Inevitability of Paraconsistency." In *Paraconsistent Logic: Essays on the Inconsistent,* edited by Graham Priest, Richard Sylvan, and Jean Norman, 177–211. Munich: Philosophia Verlag, 1989.
Prior, A. N. *Formal Logic.* Oxford: Clarendon Press, 1955.
———. *Time and Modality.* Oxford: Clarendon Press, 1957.
Putnam, Hilary. "Synonymity and the Analysis of Belief Sentences." *Analysis* 14 (1954): 114–22.
———. "On Belief Sentences: A Reply to Alonzo Church." In *Philosophy and Analysis,* edited by Margaret Macdonald. Oxford: Clarendon Press, 1954.
Quine, Willard. "Intensions Revisited." *Midwest Studies in Philosophy* 2 (1977): 5–11.
Rasmussen, S. A., and J. Ravnkilde. "Realism and Logic." *Synthese* 52 (1982): 379–437.
Rescher, Nicholas. "Presuppositions of Knowledge." *Revue Internationale de Philosophie* 12 (1959): 418–29.
———. "The Problem of a Logical Theory of Belief Statement." *Philosophy of Science* 27 (1960): 88–95.
———. "Semantic Paradoxes and the Propositional Analysis of Indirect Discourse." *Philosophy of Science* 28 (1961): 437–40.
———. *The Limits of Science,* 2nd ed. Pittsburgh, PA: University of Pittsburgh Press, 1999.
———. "Epistemic Logic." In *A Companion to Philosophical Logic,* edited by Dale Jacquette, 478–90. Oxford: Blackwell, 2002.
Rescher, Nicholas, and Arnold Vander Nat. "On Alternatives in Epistemic Logic." *Journal of Philosophical Logic* 2 (1973): 119–35.
Routley, Richard. "Necessary Limits to Knowledge: Unknown Truths." In *Essays in Scientific Philosophy,* edited by E. Morscher et al., 93–113. Bad Reichenhall: Comes, 1981.
Sainsbury, R. M. *Paradoxes.* Cambridge: Cambridge University Press, 1995.
Salmon, Nathan. *Frege's Puzzle.* Cambridge, MA: MIT Press, 1986.
Schiffer, Stephen. "Amazing Knowledge." *Journal of Philosophy* 99 (2002): 288–311.
Schlesinger, George. "On the Limits of Science." *Analysis* 46 (1986): 24–26.

Simons, P. "Vagueness and Ignorance." *Aristotelian Society* 66 (1992): 163–77.

Sorensen, Roy A. *Blindspots.* Oxford: Clarendon Press, 1988.

Stanley, Jason. "Names and Rigid Designations." In *A Companion to Philosophy of Language,* edited by Bob Hale and Crispin Wright, 555–85. Oxford: Blackwell, 1987.

Stanley, Jason, and Timothy Williamson. "Knowing How." *Journal of Philosophy* 98 (2002): 411–44.

Strawson, Peter. *Individuals.* London: Methuen, 1959.

Swain, M., ed. *Induction, Acceptance, and Rational Belief.* Dordrecht: D. Reidel, 1970.

Tuomela, Raimo. *Cooperation: A Philosophical Study.* Dordrecht: Kluwer, 2000.

van Benthem, Johan. *Modal Logic and Classical Logic.* Napoli, Italy: Grafitalia, 1983.

von Wright, G. H. *An Essay in Modal Logic.* Amsterdam: North Holland Publishing Co., 1951.

Williams, J. N. "Moore's Paradox: One or Two." *Analysis* 39, no. 3 (1979): 141–42.

Williamson, Timothy. "Intuitionism Disproved?" *Analysis* 42 (1982): 203–07.

———. "On Knowledge and the Unknowable." *Analysis* 42 (1987): 203–07.

———. "On the Paradox of Knowability." *Mind* 96 (1987): 154–58.

———. "Knowability and Constructivism." *Philosophical Quarterly* 38 (1988): 422–43.

———. *Identity and Discrimination.* Oxford: Blackwell, 1990.

———. "On Intuitionistic Modal Epistemic Logic." *Journal of Philosophical Logic* 21 (1992): 63–89.

———. "Vagueness and Ignorance." *Aristotelian Society* 66 (1992): 145–62.

———. "Verification and Non-Distributive Knowledge." *Australasian Journal of Philosophy* 71 (1993): 78–86.

———. "Definiteness and Knowability." *Southern Journal of Philosophy* 33 (1994): 171–191.

———. *Vagueness.* London: Routledge, 1994.

———. *Knowledge and Its Limits.* Oxford: Oxford University Press, 2000.

Wolgast, Elizabeth H. *Paradoxes of Knowledge.* Ithaca, NY: Cornell University Press, 1977.

Wright, Crispin. *Realism, Meaning, and Truth.* Oxford: Oxford University Press, 1987.

Yablo, Stephen. "Truth and Reflection." *Journal of Philosophical Logic* 14 (1985): 297–349.

Zemach, E. M. "Are There Logical Limits for Science?" *British Journal for the Philosophy of Science* 38 (1987): 527–32.

Ziff, Paul. *Epistemic Analysis.* Dordrecht: D. Reidel, 1984.

Index

Adams, Marilyn McCord, 130n4
Almog, Joseph, 135
Aristotle, 32, 96, 103, 120
Avogadro, Anadeo, 120

Barcan Marcus, Ruth, 135
Beall, J. C. 135
Boh, Ivan, 135
Boltzmann, Ludwig, 120

Carnap, Rudolf, 1, 125n2 (chap. 1), 135
Church, Alonzo, 2, 135
Cohen, L. J., 135

Daniels, C. B., 135
Davidson, Donald, 135
Descartes, René, 16, 111

Edgington, Dorothy, 135
Ehrlich, Philip, 129 (chap. 15)
Ellis, Brian, 135
Evans, Gareth, 135
Evans, M.G. J., 135

Fagin, Ronald, 126n1 (chap. 3), 128n4 (chap. 11), 135
Fine, Kit, 135
Fitch, Frederic B., 63, 66–70, 128n2 (chap. 12), 135
Forbes, Graeme, 136
Frege, Gottlob, 58

Girle, Rod, 136
Goldman, Alan, 126n2 (chap. 2), 136

Goodstein, R. L., 136
Grant, Ulysses S., 128n2 (chap. 11)

Halpern, Joseph Y., 126n1 (chap. 3), 135
Hardin, Russell, 136
Hart, W. D., 63, 128n3 (chap. 12), 136
Hilpinen, R., 126n2 (chap. 2), 136
Hintikka, Jaakko, 2, 136
Hiz, Henry, 125n3 (chap. 1), 136
Hodes, Harold, 136
Humberstone, I. L., 136
Husserl, Edmund, 58

Jacquette, Dale, 136

Kant, Immanuel, 95, 123
Kaplan, David, 125n6 (chap. 1)
Keynes, John Maynard, 101, 120
Kripke, Saul, 136
Kyburg, H. K. Jr., 125n2 (chap. 2), 136

Lehrer, Keith, 136
Leibniz, G. W., 110, 111
Lenzen, Wolfgang, 136
Levi, Isaac, 126n2 (chap. 2), 136
Linsky, Leonard, 136
Lloyd, A. C., 135
Łoś, Jerzy, 1, 136

MacIntosh, J. J., 63–64, 128n5 (chap. 12), 136
Massey, G. M., 126n1 (chap. 6), 136
McDowell, J. H., 135
Meinong, Alexius von, 59

Mendeleev, D., 120
Merill, B., 136
Moore, G. E., 5, 16, 125n5 (chap.1), 137
Moses, Yoram, 126n1 (chap. 3), 135

Newton, Isaac, 103, 120

Percival, Philip, 137
Planck, Max, 120
Priest, Graham, 137
Prior, Arthur N., 2, 125n3 (chap. 1), 137
Ptolemy, 120
Putnam, Hilary, 2, 137

Quine, Willard, 137

Rasmussen, S. A., 137
Ravnkilde, J., 137
Routley, Richard, 63, 137

Sainsbury, R. M., 137
Salmon, Nathan, 137
Schiffer, Stephen, 125n7 (chap. 1), 137
Schlesinger, George, 137
Simons, P., 138
Sorensen, Roy A., 126n1 (chap. 4), 127n6 (chap. 8), 129n2 (chap. 13), 138

Spade, Paul Vincent, 130n1 (chap. 16)
Spencer, Herbert, 58
Stanley, Jason, 125n7 (chap. 1), 138
Strawson, Peter, 138
Suszko, R., 125n3 (chap. 1), 136
Swain, M., 138

Tuomela, Raimo, 126n2 (chap. 6), 138

van Benthem, Johan, 138
Vander Nat, Arnold, 137
Vardi, Moshe Y., 126n1 (chap. 3), 135
von Wright, G. H., 2, 138

Wagner, Carl, 136
Williams, J. N., 138
Williamson, Timothy, 63, 125n7 (chap. 1), 128n1 (chap. 12), 138
Wittgenstein, Ludwig, 114
Wolgast, Elizabeth H., 138
Wright, Crispin, 138

Yablo, Stephen, 138

Zemach, E. M., 138
Ziff, Paul, 138